Learning to Love

People You Don't Like

Learning to Love People You Don't Like

FLOYD McCLUNG

PUBLISHING

A Ministry of Youth With A Mission

P.O. Box 55787, Seattle, WA 98155

YWAM Publishing is the publishing ministry of Youth With A Mission. Youth With A Mission (YWAM) is an international missionary organization of Christians from many denominations dedicated to presenting Jesus Christ to this generation. To this end, YWAM has focused its efforts in three main areas: 1) Training and equipping believers for their part in fulfilling the Great Commission (Matthew 28:19). 2) Personal evangelism. 3) Mercy ministry (medical and relief work).

For a free catalog of books and materials write or call:
YWAM Publishing
P.O. Box 55787
Seattle, WA 98155
(206) 771-1153

Learning to Love People You Don't Like

Published by YWAM Publishing, a division of
Youth With A Mission, P.O. Box 55787, Seattle, WA 98155.

Unless otherwise indicated, biblical quotations are from the New International Version, © New York International Bible Society 1978

RSV = Revised Standard Version, copyrighted 1946, 1952, ©1971, 1973 by the Division of Christian Education of the National Council of Churches of Christ in the USA.

ISBN 0-927545-19-5

Printed in the United States of America.

To Loren and Darlene Cunningham,
with gratitude and affection for many years of
love, trust and friendship.

Contents

I wish to express my appreciation to Geoff and Janet Benge for their inspiration and help, and to my many friends and co-workers who are still helping me learn the lessons about which I write in this book.

Last, I wish to thank Sally, Misha and Matthew for being the best family a man could ask for.

When A Word Loses
Its Meaning

"He is a great lover."
"I love you."
"I love to play football."
"I just love my new dress."
What do you do when a word loses its meaning?

How sad that a word expressing the greatest beauty and enrichment we can know has become trite through overuse.

Preachers preach about it and novelists write about it. Song-writers chant its praises and poets celebrate its joy and its pain. It is a word that communicates everything from Hollywood to heaven.

When I asked my children for help in finding the right title for this book, one of them suggested, *Not Another Mushy Book About Love.*

There seems to be one area of the Christian life, however, where love has not lost its meaning, and that is in relation to loving people whom we don't like.

When hard reality stares us in the face, especially painful reality, love rarely fails to convince us of its importance.

The true meaning of love dawns on us when we find ourselves required to love someone who has hurt us or mistreated us. Perhaps one of our greatest needs is the motivation to love such people. Or if we have given up trying, due to repeated failure, practical help.

That is the subject of this book. The Bible calls it unity; I call it "doing love." The Scriptures teach that we cannot live the Christian life with integrity unless we love people when they are impossible to get along with.

The challenge is to love and keep on loving, even when it is hard.

Are you ready?

Chapter 1

The Power of Love

In 1980, our family moved to the Red Light District of inner-city Amsterdam. Although these surroundings have become very "normal" to us now, it was a sobering decision then. We rented a cramped apartment two doors to the left of a Satanist church, and two more doors from a homosexual brothel. In Holland prostitution is legal, so when our children, Matthew and Misha, walked to school each day, they passed the large picture-glass windows where scantily dressed girls, or "women in the window" as they are known, sat waiting for their next customers.

As our children waved at the girls, and brought them special paintings they had made for them at school, these hardened women were touched in a very special way; simple, childlike acceptance can melt the hardest of hearts. Some of these very women were later to become Christians, won by the power of accepting love.

Some people who came to work with us in the Red Light District had a tough job relating to the pimps and prostitutes as fellow human beings. It is difficult to see past the sin and reach out to the sinner. But we have found the very thing that is hardest to do provides the key to sharing the Gospel with our neighbors. For if God has reached out to us in our fallen state, surely we must reach out and embrace others with His love. Although we don't condone what they're doing, we try to keep an attitude of acceptance for them as people. Sally and I have taken time to learn their names, visit them, or invite them to our home. We have found that as we accept them they have responded to us.

The difference this acceptance can have on others was highlighted for me about six months after moving into the area. A group of mission executives asked if they could see the work we were doing there. After an eye-opening walk through the narrow cobblestone streets, we started back for our apartment. On the way it occurred to me that the two very friendly prostitutes who lived next door to us could well be outside on such a lovely sunny day. I gulped as I remembered how they always greeted me by name in a warm, friendly way, which could prove embarrassing as they wore hardly any clothes.

As we turned into our street, sure enough there they were! I didn't dare look back at my conservative missionary friends as the two girls waved happily and yelled out my name. There was a wall of silence behind me. It wasn't until several months later that I found out what they really thought of that incident.

I was in the United States speaking at a missions conference when one of the members of the group approached me. He asked if I remembered the tour I gave of our "neighborhood," and after I told him I didn't, to my surprise tears welled up in his eyes.

"When you took us around the Red Light District all I could see was a mass of prostitutes, pimps and drug addicts. But when you greeted those two girls living next door to you, I was deeply moved. You called them by their names—I still remember them: Sonja and Else. It was then that I saw them as more than prostitutes—I saw them as people."

I was deeply moved. God, right there, underlined the importance of accepting others as they are, regardless of the sin in which they're involved.

Accepting Love

God loves people, not programs or good causes. He died for people, not for the cause of world evangelism. In his letter to the Romans, Paul put it this way, "God demonstrates his own love for us in this: While we were still sinners, Christ died for us" (Romans 5:8). If a holy and pure God could love us in our sinful state, then surely we can ask Him for the power to reach out to other sinners with His love. Perhaps we will have the joy of leading them into a relationship with God. Our acceptance of them could very well be the key that leads to their salvation.

By loving us, even in our rebellion against Him, God demonstrated His acceptance of us. It is accepting love which gives us the motivation and strength to repent of our selfish ways and return to Him. And it is accepting love that reassures us that He cares and understands when we fail.

Trusting Love

All those who have accepted God's forgiveness through Jesus Christ are part of a worldwide community, a brotherhood of forgiven sinners, commissioned to bring His love to others. Through us He has chosen to communicate His kindness, mercy, hope, and forgiveness. We, in essence, become God's way of saying, "I love you" to a hurt and dying world. This is a task that will keep each of us occupied for a lifetime.

How amazing that God, the Creator of the universe, has chosen to trust us with the message of His salvation. The last recorded statement of Jesus in Matthew's Gospel includes this commission: "Therefore go and make disciples of all nations, baptizing them in the name of the Father and of the Son and of the Holy Spirit, and teaching them to obey everything I have commanded you" (Matthew 28:19).

In spite of our failings and weaknesses, God has given us the most important task in the universe — proclaiming His salvation to the world. But are we always worthy of that trust? How many times have we failed Him? Yet He still believes in us and trusts us. How much more, then, do we need to trust others.

I was faced with this challenge through a young man called David. When I first met him he was discouraged and defeated, and didn't seem to have much direction in life. Some people thought it would be foolish to get involved with him, but that was because they did not see his potential. At first I didn't either. But when I thought of those who stood by me in times when I desperately needed someone to believe in me, I felt I needed to help David.

David began to share his heart for the lost and lonely young people of Amsterdam, and I caught a glimpse of a man who cared, a man who had leadership gifts and who longed for someone to believe in him. With trust and encouragement, David has become an outstanding leader. God has blessed his ministry to the youth of Amsterdam. Each week hundreds are coming to his Bible studies and many are finding Christ.

David had a lot of rough edges, and still has a few. But he has become a powerful evangelist who is reaching young people with the Gospel. Where would we be today if our brothers and sisters in Christ did not stand by us when we needed them? Trust—that is what David needed, and that is what we all need. He could have abused that trust—people sometimes do—but it was certainly worth the risk.

As Christians we are called to believe the best of each other (I Corinthians 13:7). Trusting love has the power to make people believe in themselves. It releases our true potential and turns us from discouraged failures to those who aspire to great things. It creates an atmosphere which releases creativity and stimulates the imagination. Trust motivates us to work harder than any program or set of rules could. True trust brings freedom from striving to gain acceptance, since acceptance has already been received. It produces gratefulness toward those who believe in us and wins the loyalty of hearts for a lifetime.

We often find it difficult to give a person another chance and renew our trust and faith in them. But let's not forget that God has entrusted us with the message of the Gospel. I have failed Him many times, but He was willing to pick me up and give me another chance. We must do the same for each other. Trust is the key that can unlock a person's full potential.

The Power of Healing Love

In Isaiah 53:4-5, the prophet speaks of Christ's death saying, "He took up our infirmities and carried our sorrows . . . and by his wounds we are healed." In his death Christ not only provided for the forgiveness of our sins, but also made it possible for us to be whole in mind and body.

Bob came to us as a burnt-out wreck of a man. His marriage, after fourteen years, was on the verge of total collapse, and his family business was near bankruptcy.

Among other things, he confessed a number of adulterous relationships which had left him broken and racked with guilt. Realizing the seriousness of his condition, he recommitted himself to Christ, repented of his years of unfaithfulness, and renewed the vows of faithfulness to his wife. But even then he needed healing from the wounds inflicted on his emotions by his past life of deception. Sin had etched deeply into his mind, and insecurity and guilt had taken a heavy toll. He tried to control his lying, but the years of constantly covering up sin had made lying more natural to him than telling the truth. He was frustrated by his inability to change. Bob needed what the Apostle Paul calls the "renewing of the mind" (Romans 12:2).

Sin, whether our own or another's, can scar the

emotions. But God's healing love is able to renew and restore our distorted memories and battered emotions in such a way that we no longer have to suppress our feelings of failure or carry them with us through life. God can forgive us and completely rebuild our emotions.

Think of the emotional damage done to a child who has been molested by her father from an early age. Does she have to remain a prisoner of these psychological scars all her life? No. The healing love of God can reach into the hidden memories of such a child and heal her completely.

We all, at some point, need to experience the healing balm of God's love. Throughout life people hurt us, through thoughtless comments, rejection of our work or ideas, and other ways that leave their mark on our emotions. But we are not left to ourselves, without hope. God steps into each individual situation with His healing power and gives a fresh start.

He is the great Creator and Re-Creator. He creates new beginnings for us. He draws a line behind us, and forgives everything in the past. He heals the wounds we have accumulated along the way and starts us on a new path.

God's love is the greatest power on earth today.

God's love gives hope to a despairing nation, brings embittered enemies together, restores alienated friends, unites divided churches, renews backslidden Christians, and gives us all a reason to live.

God's love can conquer the heart of the hardest criminal, change the lifestyle of a selfish pleasure-seeker, set free the most ardent terrorist, and heal the wounds of an abused child. God's love is the power that can make the difference.

The greatest act of love in human history took place when God sent His Son, Jesus, to die on the cross as a substitute for the punishment we deserved:

> This is how God showed his love among us: He sent his one and only Son into the world that we might live through him. This is love: not that we loved God, but that he loved us and sent his Son as an atoning sacrifice for our sins (I John 4:9-10).

Once we have felt the power of God's love—the way He accepts us as His children, trusts us with the most precious message in the world, and heals us of the ugly effects of sin—we will never be the same. We will want to respond to others in a way that will draw them closer to that love.

Chapter 2

Love Is Our Common Ground

I leaned forward, readjusting my position in the pew, and glanced round the room. Colonel Mc-Tagget, the American military attaché, had just strolled in, shutting the door hard behind him, keeping out the chilling Afghan wind. The click of his cowboy boots on the marble floor echoed around the room. He smiled as he greeted someone—Don Rowley I think; I could just spot his balding head over the crowd. Yes, it must be Don; there were three bedraggled, half-starved looking guys standing near him. How like Don. Whoever would have thought that short, roly-poly man would take youngsters off the street into his home to feed and clothe them? Paul Filidis sat directly opposite me; his body decorated for church with silver and turquoise rings, bracelets and necklaces. His head was bowed in prayer; a single earring dangling haplessly from his ear. Next to him sat Peter Fitzgerald. Dear Peter! What radical political views he held about caring for the poor. The Colonel and he were about as far apart as you could be when it came to politics. The atmosphere was charged with excitement as we waited for the service to begin.

There was a story to tell about each person in that room—a story of how we came to be sitting shoulder to shoulder in a church in the residential quarters of Kabul, Afghanistan. Here we were, representing twenty-one different nationalities, from Pakistanis to British and Americans; and from every end of the social, political and theological spectrum. Anyone viewing the scene from the outside, and not seeing the Bibles carried under denim-clad arms, poking out of the top of designer handbags or army surplus knapsacks, would wonder what on earth we had in common. Why would this group come together on such a cold, windy morning?

What a wonderful and unforgettable church that was! We learned to lay aside our differences and enjoy the beautiful, refreshing atmosphere of spiritual unity. This unity took time to grow and develop. We had to learn to love and accept one another, and that hadn't been easy. When we first started, it produced some explosive moments. People tried to be selective about whom they wanted to sit beside, pray with, or invite out for a meal. It was easy to simply dismiss as different someone we didn't want to get to know. But eventually our desire for fellowship drove us to acknowledge that we were one in Christ; we were all brothers and sisters in the same family.

Slowly, cold attitudes thawed as we began to relate differently to each other. At first, this was hard work, requiring openness, honesty, humility, and a determination for each of us to bring it about. However, it was something that none of us regretted doing. We had begun to relate to each other on the basis of who we were in Christ, and not on the basis of our differences. We still had our opinions, but these were no longer the basis on which we evaluated and judged one another.

When confronted with Christians who hold different views from us on a wide range of issues — from the nuclear arms' race to baptism in the Holy Spirit or the second coming of Christ—we are presented with a wonderful opportunity to check the true motives and desires of our hearts. If, for example, personal opinions about music, clothes or politics hinder us from relating to a fellow Christian, then we are forced to conclude that our opinions are more important to us than our fellowship with another brother in Christ.

Sadly, around the world today, many Christians have become so entrenched in their own opinions that they have refused the unity found in the cross of Christ, with all the healing and acceptance which that brings. We may hear of a Christian group hurling abuse at another because of their stance on, say, apartheid. But do these groups realize that in doing this, they are participating in the very same *spirit of apartheid* by rejecting those who see issues differently? It is not wrong to have differing opinions on a matter, but it is wrong to allow these opinions to divide us.

In the Western world, where too many churches have split over minor issues, many of us would do well to ask ourselves how we would fare in a country where the church is under persecution. How would we handle differences if the option of splitting off and forming a new denomination around our opinion did not exist? In the Soviet Union there are no signs like the one in front of a church which Chuck Swindoll cites: "The Original Church of God. Number Two." As Chuck says, "I don't know whether that makes God laugh or cry!"[1]

Questions of doctrine are important, but never so important that we refuse to have fellowship with other Christians—unless they blatantly deny one of the essentials of the Christian faith.

Most Christians would agree with the saying, "In the essentials let there be unity, in the nonessentials let there be liberty, and in all things let there be charity."

Christian unity is built on the foundation of fellowship with other forgiven sinners. No more is required for doctrinal unity than agreement on the essentials. The question that arises is, "What are the essentials?"

In I Corinthians 15:1-5, Paul lists those doctrinal issues he considers to be of "first importance," or essential, to the Christian faith.

- Christ died for our sins.

- He is the Christ of the Old Testament Scriptures, which means He is the Son of God.

- He was raised on the third day and appeared to the disciples.

There are many important doctrines Paul did not include in his list, and some very important "anti-doctrines" or heresies that he did not mention, either. His list is not complete by any means. But it is enough for Biblical unity.

Imitation Unity

To attempt to manufacture Christian love and unity is ultimately to destroy it. True unity comes as a result of Christ's work on the cross and in our hearts. When we accept His love and forgiveness through the cross, we become brothers or sisters of all those who have done the same.

However, not everyone is willing to accept this kind of unity. Instead, they try to create it in human ways, by their own efforts. There are two ways in which Christians try to "create unity."

1. Legalism

Unity must never be confused with uniformity. The latter occurs when teachings in God's Word that are relative to a particular culture or set of circumstances are applied to all men for all time. It also occurs when truth is applied in a harsh and unloving manner. The end product is not righteousness but legalism.

Legalism is putting trust in the letter of truth rather than in the principles underlying that truth. There are many forms of legalism, from rules of doctrine, church government and moral conduct to regulations of musical tastes, dress, and even food. Although it is right to have our own personal convictions in various areas, it is wrong for us to insist on agreement in these areas as the basis for fellowship and loving acceptance. To do so not only denies God's grace as the only means of salvation, but also creates our own rules for holiness and spirituality. We become like the Pharisees of Jesus' day: so concerned with their own interpretation of the law that they were blind to the Messiah, and hindered others from seeing Him too. Legalism causes us to become unloving and judgmental, especially if we apply God's moral laws to those weak areas of people's lives in a harsh, unloving way.

It is not necessarily wrong to have rules that govern various areas of our lives. But what often happens is that the more rules we have, the more freedom we feel to attack and break fellowship with those who do not keep them.

Many sects attempt to find unity by establishing a list of rules and doctrines and demanding that they be maintained or adhered to with unquestioning allegiance. But this is not Biblical unity, it is uniformity. It actually destroys real unity which comes only through the work of the Holy Spirit at the cross. Real unity is not based on agreement on doctrine, or by dressing and behaving in a certain fashion, like so many puppets marching to a tune set by some self-appointed spiritual dictator. In fact, Jesus left His disciples few rules to follow. What He desired was obedience from the heart. Obviously, He affirmed the moral aspects of the law, but the legalistic application of the law made Him more angry than any sin He confronted.

Real unity is dependent on the work of the Spirit in our hearts. It is a result of building our lives on the essentials of the faith (mentioned above) and having a right attitude toward others in the Body of Christ.

The spiritual unity described in John 17 can only come when there is freedom for diversity. If we are not mature enough to disagree with each other and yet still love one another without suspicion and mistrust, we do not have sound doctrine. Sound doctrine may exclude many things, but it always includes love from the heart toward our brothers and sisters in the Lord. The concept that sound doctrine relates to our character may be new to some, but a careful study of Paul's letters to Timothy will help clarify this. Note especially I Timothy 1:8-11; 4:11-16; 6:3-10, and II Timothy 3:12-14.

2. Liberalism

The second way we try to create unity is by denying the absolutes of God's Word. If legalism is making the *relative* teachings of God's Word *absolute*, then liberalism is making the *absolute* truths of His Word *relative*. The motivation for doing this is the fear that any doctrine or teaching that tends to be exclusive may offend or hinder those we want to include as a "brother."

However, there are some truths in God's Word that are absolutely true for all men for all time. These include the deity of Christ, salvation through faith in His death on the cross, and belief in the bodily resurrection of Christ. In their desire for the brotherhood of all men, some deny the absoluteness of some of the teachings of God's Word. They may teach, for example, that all men are God's children, be they Buddhists, Muslims, or agnostics. Directly or indirectly they deny that the only way to the Father is through Jesus Christ. However the Scriptures make it abundantly clear that salvation and eternal life come only through faith in our Lord Jesus, and confession of our sins (John 14:6; 17:1-3; Acts 4:12).

Some compromise the foundational truths of Christianity in order to tolerate and accept all religions. But in doing this they become intolerant of anyone who preaches the cross as God's provision for the salvation of all mankind. Others compromise certain aspects of the Bible's moral teaching, such as the practice of sex only within marriage. This is sometimes done to be more "loving" towards young people or to those involved in homosexuality. When we compromise God's standards, we actually are being unloving. The way to truly love someone in these situations is to help them see, and break through, the sin that binds their personalities and distorts their relationships.

Anyone who gets sexually involved outside marriage is going to get hurt. God created us to give ourselves sexually in marriage to a life partner of the opposite sex. Violation of the way God intended us to live does not bring freedom but bondage, and not to tell others of this is unloving.

Through many years of working with young people in Afghanistan and Amsterdam, I have had a number of opportunities to become friends with people who were ignorant of, or disobedient to, God's laws regarding sexual purity. I remember confronting one young couple about why it was wrong to live together outside of marriage. We talked about trust, and how that can only come with public commitment to an exclusive, lifelong relationship. We discussed God's plan for secure, happy families and how this can never be achieved without such commitment. The bond between them gradually dissolved as they honestly faced up to the selfish and superficial nature of their relationship.

Today both of them are Christians, happily married to other people and actively serving the Lord. They often thank me for helping them face the sin in their lives. Hitting them over the head with the Bible wouldn't have worked, but sharing openly with them why God asks us to be totally committed to another person in marriage did. With God's help I achieved a balance of tenderness and directness that let them know I was deeply committed to them while challenging them about inconsistency in their lives. It is possible to uphold a biblical standard and be loving at the same time.

God gave us the Ten Commandments for our good. To disobey them is to not only go against a set of moral laws but the very character of God. He created us in His image to live in consistency with His great character. When we break one of the Ten Commandments we are not just breaking one of His laws, which is significant enough, but we are violating the character of God as revealed in His moral law.

While we can experience a high degree of love and acceptance for our fellow men, it is not possible to share Christian unity with a person unless he has acknowledged his sin and need of forgiveness by the Lord Jesus.

Both legalism and liberalism destroy true Christian unity and make it difficult to have real love for other believers. One adds to what Christ has done, while the other subtracts. If we are to experience true spiritual unity, it must come through the Holy Spirit and not the flesh.

Loving Difficult People

When it comes right down to it, we need a good reason to love some people—a very good reason! It often seems much easier just to avoid them. Haven't you ever asked yourself, "Why bother? If he goes his way and I go mine, then we can avoid a lot of unnecessary conflict."

Most of us are busy enough as it is, without having the extra burden of working through relationship problems that could be better handled by just staying out of each other's hair. It seems easier just to chalk it up to a natural personality conflict. Anyway, some people are so strange that no one could possibly get along with them. Right?

Wrong! Deep in our hearts we know the right thing to do—we must face difficult relationships and work through them. After all, if these "difficult people" are Christians we will have to live with them when we get to heaven, so why not get a head start?

Bear with me for a moment's poetic license . . . imagine how embarrassing if you were called up in front of everyone on Judgment Day along with the person you have been avoiding all of your life. In front of everyone gathered around the throne Jesus asks, "Why haven't you two worked this out? Go to the room over there on your right, and don't come back until you have taken care of this thing once and for all!"

To love people we don't like is one of life's great challenges. It takes extra motivation and help from outside ourselves. For me, the greatest motivation to love people I don't like is God's love for me. When we struggle in our response to another person, we must remember that we are all sinners whom God has forgiven for many things. If we cannot forgive others for their sins against us, then perhaps we have lost sight of just how much we have been forgiven.

Pride always causes us to look down on others; to think that we are better than someone else. By its very nature pride is deceptive. But we can gain a new understanding from God of our sinfulness and our desperate need to humble ourselves, returning to Him in an attitude of weakness. Only in this state, which some call "brokenness," can we find the resources to love another human being. Love for one another must be our common ground.

Sin, and our need of forgiveness, is the great equalizer. Jesus does not divide sinners into categories; the nice ones on this side and the nasty ones on the other. He does not build platforms at the cross so some of us are closer to Him. All of us share one common characteristic: sin. Baptist sinners, Episcopalian sinners, Reformed sinners, Pentecostal sinners, Roman Catholic sinners—all of us stand together at the foot of the cross.

It is, however, is not the common characteristic of sin that makes it possible to love one another and enjoy unity, though a little dose of humility never hurts. It is the cross that unites us. Through the cross of Christ we are forgiven and accepted, and because we are forgiven, we can forgive and accept others.

Despite our rebellion against God, He has loved us with an unimaginable love. He created us. We rebelled against Him, but He responded by sending His Son to die for us.

This profound truth was brought home to me while I was visiting friends from South Africa who had recently adopted twins. I asked Don and Cecelia what they had learned by adopting children, especially since they had adopted a little girl two years previously. I'll never forget Don's reply: "We've learned that love is thicker than blood."

Not fully understanding what Don had meant, I asked him to explain. He related how the Lord had led them to study passages of Scripture that dealt with the concept of adoption, even though the verses were primarily related to God's love for us, and not about us adopting children. Through studying these passages, Don and Cecelia discovered that not being God's "natural" children means He chooses us to be His children simply because He wants us. We have received the "full rights of sons" (Galatians 4:5). We have been adopted, chosen by God to belong to Him.

Just because children are born to two people does not mean they are wanted. They need to be chosen from the heart, loved and welcomed. In the same way, we need to "adopt" one another. We are to love one another as our heavenly Father has loved us. In this way, love is thicker than blood. We can be as close, and in some cases much closer, than natural brothers and sisters.

1.   Charles Swindoll, *Growing Strong in the Seasons of Life,* Multnomah Press, 1983.

Chapter 3

Unity—Love In Action

There is nothing more painful than a church split. Nothing is more damaging than a congregation torn apart by mistrust, backbiting and factions. Many Christians carry the memory of at least one such split: a memory that lingers on, even after many years.

I well remember one church that was divided after the pastor's adulterous involvement with several of the elders' wives. Two of the elders had committed suicide, and strife reigned throughout the church. The newspapers picked up the story, and for months Christ's name was dragged through the mud. Non-Christians just shook their heads and vowed never to attend church again, anywhere.

In another church situation I encountered, theology was the prime reason for a split. The issue was so minor that I cannot even remember what it was. However, I still have vivid recollections of the bitterness it generated.

In Holland, one denomination has been formed

as a result of an argument about the mode of infant baptism. A great dispute erupted about the right formula to use when baptizing little babies!

Perhaps you've heard the saying, "If you have one believer you have a Christian, if you have two believers you have a church, and if you have three believers you have two churches." Perhaps it's too close to the truth to be funny.

Unity in all our relationships

If you have never been involved in such a split, you may be thinking, "What has unity got to do with me?"

Love and unity form the basis on which God wants us to relate in *every* situation, and His name is at stake whenever there is disunity in the Church. You and I are His Church. Jesus tells us that "where two or three come together in my name, there am I with them" (Matthew 18:20). Even when we are outside the "church setting" at home with our family, or with Christian friends and acquaintances, we are still His Church. Are all our various relationships marked by love and unity, or do strife and devision creep in? Do we love and encourage our children, or are we often at odds with them? Are we genuinely concerned about the well-being of other Christians at work, or are we only concerned about ourselves — our vindication in a matter, our happiness and fulfillment?

Love and unity should be at the heart of every relationship in which we Christians are involved. The Bible tells us we are to love all men and live in unity with our fellow believers.

As a husband I must love my wife, Sally, and actively seek to live in unity with her. We are the Church in our home, and Christ has promised to dwell in our midst. Unity is not something that comes automatically when two people are married; it has to be worked at. Sally and I share the responsibility to seek unity in every area of our marriage.

When we were first married I thought it would be simple. After all, we knew each other so well. How wrong I was! I soon discovered that we had each married an idealized version of who the other really was. I said "I do" to a combination of Elizabeth Taylor, Mother Teresa, and Betty Crocker! But worse still, as far as I was concerned, she imagined me as the best parts of John Wayne, Billy Graham, and Charles Atlas! Not surprisingly, our first two years of marriage were at times stormy, as we learned to adjust and relate to each other on the basis of who we really were, and not some idealized view. Part of the problem was our pride. We did not want to admit we had married someone who was less than perfect (though it must have been obvious to others).

As Christians we often idealize fellow believers in the same way, putting them on pedestals, only to be hurt and embittered when they fail to live up to our expectations. We must come to the place where, in an attitude of love, we can embrace one another while still acknowledging one another's faults. Refusing to accept each other in this way may well lead us to becoming the policemen of the church—judgmental and critical.

In our marriage I had to learn that I could not act as the Holy Spirit, bringing conviction to Sally when and where I thought necessary. That is God's job. God has charged me to love and cherish my wife and be a living example of His character for her (Ephesians 5:25). I am not called to be her judge. If there are areas of weakness in her life, then I am to pray for her and allow God to bring conviction to her heart—and she must do the same for me.

In our relationships with other Christians, we often lose sight of this principle. We are busy trying to bring conviction to those with whom we do not agree, or to those who have some obvious fault that we feel needs correcting. But instead of helping, we bring disharmony.

It is essential that love takes prime place in our relationships. Where there are differences, we must reach out in love to our brother and allow the Holy Spirit to do His convicting work in both our lives. He, after all, is the only one who is able to do this justly, since He knows the thoughts and intents of our heart.

As a father, I also need to seek unity with my two children. Just because they are my children, living in my home, does not permit me to dispense with the principles of love and unity. I cannot rant at them, belittle their feelings and ideas, or do anything that makes them feel less significant or worthwhile than I. Matthew and Misha may belong to a different generation than mine, but they are my brother and sister in Christ. One day we will stand as equals in Christ's presence. I am expected to live in unity with them as fellow believers. This is not always easy, but I have to release them from my expectations and allow them to be themselves—a principle that holds true for every relationship.

This concept of love and its relationship to unity, affects every area of a Christian's life. We know from

Scripture that Jesus intercedes for us (Hebrews 7:25), but there is only one record of exactly what He prays for us, His church:

> My prayer is not for them alone. I pray also for those who will believe in me through their message, *that all of them may be one* . . . May they be brought to complete unity to let the world know that you sent me and have loved them even as you have loved me (John 17:20-21, 23; my italics).

Disunity and division in any part of the Body of Christ is a scandal that non-Christians are eager to file away as a reason for not taking the Gospel seriously. Every time we participate in a church quarrel, practice disunity, are unloving towards each other, or in any way participate in actions and attitudes that lead to division or mistrust, we raise a barrier that can keep relatives, friends and business associates from faith in Christ. Involvement in this way only confirms to them what they already suspect — Christianity is a religion of hypocrites.

Divorce — the ultimate form of disunity

In Britain today one in every three couples getting married are heading for divorce, while in the United States it is now one in every two. What a tragic statistic! In Malachi 2:16, God expresses His hatred of divorce — the breaking of unity between two people who have made a binding commitment to each other. How He must grieve over the consequences of this disunity.

Divorce is like throwing a stone into a pond—the ripples get wider and wider. It's not only the husband and wife who suffer, but also the children. Psychologists tell us that despite much reassurance to the contrary, many children carry with them the guilt that they are in some way responsible for the break-up of their parents' marriage.

Society at large also suffers. A recently released statistic in the United States showed that 89% of all spontaneous violent crimes—rape, murder, assault, etc.—were committed by people from single-parent homes. No wonder God hates divorce.

Although the ripples of divorce are felt throughout society, I believe the opposite also holds true. Christian families, churches and organizations that dwell in unity have a positive, stabilizing effect on society. This should challenge each of us to love one another more deeply and seek unity more actively.

I believe that disunity in the Body of Christ is akin to spiritual divorce from our brother. We have broken the commitment to love and accept one another—the commitment God expects us to live by. In breaking this commitment we fall prey to hurt, bitterness, mistrust, alienation and many other things that sap our spiritual life and wreak havoc in the Body of Christ.

Many of us, because of personal disappointments, no longer believe that biblical unity is possible. Consequently, our perception of God's Word is blurred, causing us to focus on our hurts and frustrations. But God is greater than our hurtful experiences. We must not allow unbelief to rule our hearts.

Unbelief is the darkroom of our life, where doubts and fears develop into negatives!

While reading these words, perhaps some painful memories have been stirred up. If so, do not just read on without taking time to talk to God about your hurts. Confess them to the Lord, asking for His healing, then forgive those who have hurt you. As you do so, maybe over a period of time, God will release hope and love into your heart.

Jesus prayed for what was possible

Biblical unity is not easy to achieve. I am the first to admit that it is no simple task to love others and build unity. My father is a pastor, and during my childhood we moved to four or five different churches that had experienced major divisions and splits.

Dad's role was a peacemaker. Patiently he would talk first with one side and then the other. He would listen to their grievances, negotiate, and bring the Holy Spirit's healing into the various situations. Brick by brick, he would help pull down walls that divided. Believe me, I grew up with little idealism about church unity!

Now, as a leader in Youth With A Mission, I am called upon to help promote unity in many different circumstances. This mission has an extremely diverse range of nationalities, denominations, ages and backgrounds. With such a varied group, the potential for conflict, misunderstanding and disunity is enormous. Yet many times it has been my privilege to see tensions worked through and overcome by applying biblical principles, and a commitment to the conviction that we are called to live as Christian brothers and sisters in love and unity.

Unity is possible. Would Jesus bother to pray for something that was not possible? Would He be so cruel as to raise our hopes and give us the expectation that we, as His church, can live in deep love, fellowship and trust, only to disappoint and disillusion us?

Jesus prays for unity despite political, social and age differences, and despite the cultural and racial barriers behind which we hide. He prays for a unity that will transcend denominationalism and, in some cases, our thick-walled "non-denominationalism!" Relationship conflicts, independence, demanding our rights, leading or participating in church arguments, and taking part in church splits are all sins that are in direct opposition to the prayer Jesus prayed in John 17.

Many people are concerned about who is right when there is division in the church, but no one who participates in division is right. It is not a matter of who is right, but who is obedient to God's word. The issues that divide us may be important, but there is something higher on God's list of priorities — and that is unity.

You may have to leave a church because of division that is simply beyond your control. Division is sometimes the result of intransigence on the part of an offending person; if there is no heartfelt repentance, a split may result over which you have no control. You may also be forced to distance yourself from a situation simply because it is so bad. Whenever such a situation arises, we must be certain that our motives are pure and that we are not using the wrongs of others as an excuse to vent anger and resentment in the name of righteous indignation.

Love one another!

Unity is only possible if we love one another. The implication in Jesus' prayer for unity is that love is absolutely essential if we are to please Him.

In John 17:23, Jesus prays that we will be one so that the world will know the Father has loved us *in the same way as He has loved the Son*. The Father loves you and me as much as He loves His own Son. What amazing love! Our love for one another can enable people to see and experience the Father's love. Some wonder why so many lonely, hurting people are attracted to them as Christians. We should never be ashamed of the fact that the lonely and unlovely want to be around us; they are attracted to the love of the Father they see manifested in us.

What is referred to in John 17 is clearly spelled out in John 15. There, Jesus *commands* us to love one another. Some may dismiss their obligation to love others outlined in John 17, because it is set out in the form of a prayer. But two chapters earlier, Jesus says that there is no other option for the Christian. It's a command. We must love one another. Whether we make excuses or not, Jesus makes it very clear how He expects us to relate to one another.

Unity is not only possible, it is absolutely essential. If we believe that what Jesus prays for us is possible, and that He will accept nothing less than our total, heartfelt obedience, then we are cornered. No more excuses or rationalizations. If we choose to follow Jesus, we must do so on His terms, not ours.

The nature of love

There is a lot of confusion about the nature of love. Is it some mushy feeling that comes over us, making us starry-eyed as so many films portray? A closer study of John 15 gives more understanding of the word love.

In verses 13 to 17, Jesus defines the true nature of love:

- It is *sacrificial.*

    We are to die to what we want for the sake of others. Sometimes I think it would actually be easier to die for someone than to live for them. But Jesus requires us to die to our rights, preferences and desires and to live for others.

- It is *choosing* to do what is right.

    "You are my friends if you obey me," Jesus says. Love is much more than a feeling. It is choosing to do and think what is right, even when we don't feel like it.

- It is *openness* to freely share our thoughts and feelings.

    Jesus told his disciples that they were not servants but friends, because He shared everything with them.

- It is *commitment.*

  Jesus told the disciples that He chose them not because they chose Him, but because He wanted them to be His friends and fellow workers.

- It is *trust.*

  Jesus trusted the disciples and sent them out to represent Him and the Father.

- It is *obedience* to a higher purpose in life — that of living for the Lord and others first.

We are commanded to love one another, but the idea of being told what to do runs against our grain. The sinful part of man, what the Bible calls our "flesh," fights for every opportunity to avoid dealing with the idea of living our lives for others first. We look for every chance to avoid loving people that, from our small perspective, are unlovely.

Until we accept the fact that the Lord Jesus demands our unconditional obedience, we will continue to come up with all kinds of rationalizations to avoid obeying Him. Not until we believe with all our hearts that we must obey Him, will we do it. And then only with His help.

We must bow our hearts before Him and acknowledge how selfish we are at the very core of our being. When we see that it's foreign to love others in the way Jesus prayed for in John 17 and commanded in John 15, the Holy Spirit can begin to work in us and enable us to do it. This kind of honesty with God allows us to receive into our hearts the love He wants us to have for others.

The supreme example of love

Did you notice that in John 17, Jesus prayed that the love we have for one another would be like the love He and the Father have for each other? How do they love each other? Understanding the love between the Father and the Son will help us to understand further the true nature of love.

When Jesus came to earth He gave up all His heavenly privileges and rights (Philemon 2:6-8). He submitted to the will of the Father (Matthew 26:36-46). He was open with the Father, sharing His feelings honestly and yet without any manipulation (Mt. 26:39). He honored the Father in everything He did (John 8:28-29).

The Father loved the Son, honoring Him publicly as His beloved Son (Mark 1:11). He trusted the Son with the greatest responsibility of all time—the redemption of mankind (John 3:16). He shared everything with Him (John 17:6-26).

This same relationship of love, trust and honor is offered to us. Jesus prays that we will love each other in the same manner as He and the Father love one another.

The question remains, "How does this work out in reality?" Jesus said it was possible, but are there steps we can follow to help us love one another in our daily life?

Chapter 4

Rules For Relationships

Many people are waiting for those around them to become perfect, while others look for a perfect church. But expecting perfection in a fallen world will only set us up for disappointment and heartache. Unity in a fallen world does not imply the total absence of evil and sin, nor does it mean absolute doctrinal purity. What unity does mean is that we have a Christlike attitude towards others when they do sin or when they are wrong, since we have placed our faith in Christ for the forgiveness of our own sins.

In Ephesians, chapters 4 and 5, Paul describes the principles and attitudes we must have to guard the unity given to us through Jesus' death on the cross. In chapter 4 he tells us to be "eager to maintain the unity of the Spirit in the bond of peace . . . until we all attain to the unity of the faith and of the knowledge of the Son of God, to mature manhood, to the measure of the stature of the fulness of Christ" (Ephesians 4:3,13 RSV).

Paul compares unity of the Spirit (having the right attitude of heart and mind towards one another in spite of weakness or sin) with unity of the faith (absolute maturity and doctrinal perfection). He challenges the Church to be eager to maintain the unity of the Spirit until we attain the unity of the faith.

This implies three things. First, unity of the Spirit must be our priority until God brings His church to the unity of the faith. Secondly, we must be eager to *maintain* the unity of the Spirit. And thirdly, we must not insist on unity of the faith (spiritual maturity and doctrinal purity) as the basis for loving others. To do so is a work of the flesh and, as such, sin.

Are we eager to forgive those who hurt us, accept those who are different from us, prefer those who disagree with us, love those who attack us, submit to those over us, trust those who lead us, go to those who hurt us, and be patient with those who disagree with us? If not, we need to repent. We need to ask God for a deeper revelation of our heart, of the sin that keeps us from wanting that degree of love and unity. We're not talking about a feeling, but a basic attitude. Unity begins with an attitude of heart that is the fruit of brokenness in our lives. God does not want us to be the judge of other people's hearts and lives. He wants us to judge our own. It's when we lose that brokenness and become hard and judgmental that we lose our eagerness for unity.

Practical rules for building relationships

We should not wonder why other people are wrong or

have sinned. We should consider how we're going to respond to them. Will we demand unreasonable conditions before they are restored to fellowship, or will we respond with quick and joyful forgiveness?

The following checklist will help test our motives in this area. Please read this list prayerfully, and ask the Holy Spirit to speak to you as you do so.

(1) Paul tells us in Ephesians 4:2 that we must maintain an attitude of humility, meekness, patience and forbearance. Such an attitude, maintained in our everyday life, gives greatest power.

- *Humility* means we are willing to be known for who we are and for what we have done, rather than building relationships on a superficial level. It means we are prepared to do anything necessary to make matters right with others when we have sinned against them or hurt them.

- *Meekness* means we will not insist on doing things our way or pushing ourselves forward.

- *Patience* means we wait for others lovingly, even when they are wrong.

- *Forbearance* means we help others when they are weak.

(2) We are to speak the truth in love (Ephesians 4:15, 25, 26, 29-31). Paul gives a great deal of attention to the tongue, telling us several things about our speech which we need to note carefully.

Do you want to keep your friendships? Do you

want your relationships to glorify Christ? Then:

- Speak the *truth*. We are to be direct, forthright and honest.

- Speak the truth *in love*. We are not to speak in anger, bitterness or an unkind manner, but in God's timing, waiting for Him to prepare the hearts of those to whom we are going to speak. It also implies we should be selective about what we do say; a wise person does not divulge everything he knows.

- Only speak that which *edifies*. In other words, only say things which are positive and helpful. It is not enough to excuse ourselves by saying, "I was only being honest." You can completely devastate someone by being ruthlessly honest with them at the wrong time. The issue is greater than honesty; the Bible teaches that we should only say those things that will help a person. Honesty without wisdom can be sin.

- Get rid of a *critical spirit*. "Let all bitterness and wrath and anger and clamor and slander be put away from you," Paul exhorts the Ephesians (Ephesians 4:31 RSV). The root of all these is a critical spirit, one of the great enemies of unity. Do you find it easier to criticize someone than to encourage him? Repeating people's faults and sins to others is classified as a sin in the Bible, as it spreads mistrust and encourages division. It is poison that can quickly infect the whole body.

Several years ago I was in a meeting where leaders had gathered to discuss some cooperative efforts towards unity in the Body of Christ. Someone put forward the name of a leader whom they felt should be invited to join the meeting. In reply to this, a pastor announced that some of the people in his church had had dealings in the past with him and said he was not a good man.

When the objecting pastor was pressed further on the issue, he admitted that he did not know the leader in question personally, and had not questioned the members of his congregation about their opinion of him. More importantly, he had never bothered to seek reconciliation between the members of his congregation and this leader.

This is sin. He was sowing seeds of doubt and mistrust in our minds through an unsubstantiated and unresolved conflict. The breakdown in unity between his church members and this leader could easily have led to a breakdown among us as well.

Slander, if it goes unchecked, breeds disunity. Even if something is true, it is not necessary to say it publicly, unless it has to do with moral compromise or serious doctrinal error. God calls us to be accountable for what we say, to be loyal to one another, and to promote reconciliation, forgiveness and unity. This is not an optional extra for "mature" Christians. We are all commanded to do it.

(3) Paul exhorts believers to forgive those who sin and to discipline those who do not repent of their sins (Ephesians 4:32; 5:1; 5:5-7).

There can be no unity without forgiveness and

church discipline. There is no problem of disunity that cannot be solved by greater humility or forgiveness. When there is no humility evident on the part of a brother who has sinned, there should be gentle but firm discipline. Whether men repent or not, we are to forgive them. But when they fail to repent, even though we forgive them, church leaders should lovingly bring discipline into their lives.

(4) We must acknowledge that we belong to one another. Everyone who belongs to Jesus is a member of our family, a coheir of His grace. Just as in a normal family, there are some members who get along better and have more in common with each other. So it is in God's family. In our earthly families we don't deny someone is our brother or sister simply because he or she is different from us. Neither should we do that in the Church, for we are members of one another (Ephesians 4:25).

I remember telling a friend that there was one group of Christians with whom I could never work or be publicly identified. I felt that their doctrine was so bad and their evangelistic practices so poor that they were a disgrace to the Lord's name. It would have been an embarrassing compromise for me to be identified with them. I went on to tell my friend that I believed they were Christians but thought they were very wrong and I hated what they stood for and the way they expressed their faith. They weren't stealing, lying, or denying the deity of Christ, but I just "knew" their superficial practices were hurting the Lord.

My friend told me I had a problem, and it was pride. What a shock! I thought I was so righteous, so biblically sound in my beliefs and practices. After the initial indignation wore off, I asked the Lord to show me if I were wrong. Immediately I began to think of how much Christ loved me in spite of my many sins and failures, to the point of welcoming me into His family and giving me His name. If the Son of God was able to identify with me, a member of the sinful human race, why was I unable to identify with these other believers?

Ironically, the more I got to know the people in that particular group, the more I liked them. My pride had blinded me and kept me from seeing what they had to teach me. Perhaps our prejudices against other Christian groups reflect our blind spots—the places where we are weakest and most need them to help us grow.

There is only one Church. However, judging from our behavior one would think that we seriously believe that when we get to heaven God will divide us into different sections so we can huddle together within our little group or denomination. Worse still, some behave as if their group will be the only one there. But when we do get to heaven we will all be one, so why not get a head start and begin getting to know Christians of other denominations and groups right now? Let's lay aside our sectarianism, fear and pride, and reach out to one another—after all, we belong to one another.

It was Count Zinzendorf of the Moravians who taught that God does not reveal all His truth to any one person or Christian group. He believed that God had distributed knowledge of biblical truth to all groups so that we would be dependent upon one another for balance and protection. If we could really grasp this insight—especially those of us who are leaders—our attitude towards one another would be very different.

(5) Lastly, Paul exhorts us to be filled with the Spirit, worshiping the Lord, encouraging one another, and always giving thanks in everything to God the Father.

Gratefulness. Encouragement. Thanksgiving. Such qualities are not accidentally acquired. They need to be deliberately cultivated until they become part of our daily thought patterns and actions. We need to spend time in God's presence, asking Him how to encourage those around us. We need to also ask Him for a fresh revelation of all He has done, and provided for us; then our hearts will be full of thankfulness.

When we finally come to a place of dwelling in unity, what a blessing that is! It makes everything worthwhile.

> How good and pleasant it is
>   when brothers live together in unity!
> It is like precious oil poured on the
>   head,
>   running down on the beard,
> running down on Aaron's beard,
>   down upon the collar of his robes.
> It is as if the dew of Hermon
>   were falling on Mount Zion,
> For there the Lord bestows his blessing,
>   even life forevermore (Psalm 133).

Chapter 5

"Even Sinners Do That!"

Several years ago, there was a popular Christian chorus that really bothered me. One line, in fact about the only line in the entire song, went like this: "Jesus in me loves you." Depending on the particular worship leader, we were supposed to either look around the room and smile at each other, hug the person on our left, or greet eighteen people we hadn't met before—all while singing the song! At those times I resented my six-foot-plus height which made it impossible to mingle inconspicuously.

I was irritated because I couldn't fathom how merely singing a song proved we loved each other. I already knew Jesus loved me, but simply repeating a jingle didn't convince me that the man in the next pew loved me. Perhaps if we had been asked to get our wallets out and bless each other financially while we sang, the song would have been more convincing! But I fear in that case there would have been a few ashen-faced worshipers heading for the exits.

It's easy to become super-spiritual about love,

and fail to think through what it really means. Jesus said, "If you love those who love you, what credit is that to you? Even 'sinners' love those who love them. And if you do good to those who are good to you, what credit is that to you? Even 'sinners' do that" (Luke 6:32-33).

So, if we love friends and family because they love us in return, or if we return a favor someone has done for us, so what? Anyone can do that—whether he has God's love in his heart or not. Jesus implies that we are not to expect any great reward if we love only on that level.

What about loving the person who rips us off in a business deal and then takes Communion with us on Sunday? How about the one who has a sharp tongue and is constantly wounding us with cruel and sarcastic comments? Or the boss who does not trust us and won't give us the opportunities we need to prove ourselves? Jesus makes it clear in Luke 6 that real love has not even begun until it is sacrificial, until it cuts against the grain of our fallen nature. He commands us to love our enemies and bless those who abuse and speak against us. When people hate us, we are not to respond to them in that same spirit. When they slander us, we must speak positively about them. And when they use us, we must give to them.

It is ironic that the thing which is hardest to do—loving someone who is truly difficult—is the very means by which Jesus promises that He will put His mark on us. "All men will know that you are my disciples if you love one another" (John 13:35). Perhaps you are thinking, "I can't forgive so-and-so for letting me down like he did. It's just not humanly possible." Agreed, but who said that we are limited to human resources when loving others? "The one who is in you is greater than the one who is in the world" (I John 4:4). We serve someone who wants to show the world superhuman love through us.

It is going beyond the ordinary into the extraordinary that marks us as Jesus' disciples. Living in Amsterdam, we had the privilege of getting to know Corrie ten Boom, or Tante Corrie as we affectionately came to call her. After she had been to visit us, I would often walk back with her along the canals to her car. As we walked she would tell me about Holland during the German occupation. She and her family had been responsible for smuggling many Jews out of the country, and when their scheme was finally discovered, she, her sisters Betsie and Nollie, brother Willem and her father were sent to concentration camp. Her father only survived ten days, but Corrie had the agony of watching life seep slowly from Betsie as she was beaten and abused by SS guards.

After the war, Corrie began spreading God's message of forgiveness all over Europe. She proclaimed that there is nothing we have done that God cannot forgive. As we walked together one afternoon, she told me of the time when this very message was tested in her life.

She had been speaking at a church in Munich when afterwards, one of the SS guards from the concentration camp in which Betsie and Corrie had been interred came up to speak with her. Memories flooded her mind of Betsie's emaciated body having the last drop of usefulness wrung from it. She well remembered this guard as he stretched forth his hand to shake hers. He smilingly agreed with her message that God forgives all our sins. Corrie related that it felt like an eternity before she found the grace from God to extend her hand to the guard. As she did, the warmth of God's love flooded her as she began to feel His love for the man.

She told me that audiences responded the most to this story of shaking that man's hand. People would exclaim, "I could never do that. It would be too much!" Yet they still wanted to hear the story. Why? Because the things which we cannot achieve in our own strength or goodness of heart inspire us and convince the unbeliever that God lives.

We must apply the Gospel to our daily lifestyle, and refuse to treat people the way they have treated us. Jesus tells us that we are to love our enemies and pray for those who despitefully use us. But who are our enemies, and how do we love them in practical terms?

Enemies—the word conjures up images of Hitler, armored tanks, and muggers lurking behind bushes. But the word has a much broader meaning, and it is to this that Jesus referred when He spoke of loving our enemies.

One of the meanings that Webster's dictionary gives to the word "enemy" is: "One that seeks the injury, overthrow, or failure of an opponent. One who shows hostility, ill will, or has hatred or a destructive attitude." Many people whom we know fall into this category at various times, whether they seek our physical, psychological, emotional, or spiritual injury. Sometimes even those in our family show ill will towards us, or harbor a destructive attitude against us. Are there practical steps we can take that will help us to love these people as Jesus wants us to love them?

Love always begins with humility

"For all have sinned and fall short of the glory of
God" (Romans 3:23). Let's apply this verse to ourselves before we start using it to point the finger at
others. When we lose sight of how unlovable we have
been at times, we become proud and self-righteous. It
becomes much easier to love an unloving person
when we are conscious of our own failures.

An acquaintance of mine was traveling down the
freeway one day, complaining to the Lord about his
troubles. He felt that many people were criticizing
him unfairly, even fabricating lies to bolster their
case. He was crying out for sympathy and
understanding, so he was very surprised when he felt
the Lord say, "Just be glad they don't know the real
truth about you!"

Too often we tend to see the good in ourselves
and remember our successes rather than our failures.
So let's treat others the same way—remember, "Love
your neighbor as yourself" (Matthew 22:39).

Forgive those who hurt and irritate you

Forgiveness is not a feeling. Neither is it simply
trying to forget the bad things done to us. It is an act
of the will and heart. It is giving a person something
they have not earned the right to have—pardon. Forgiveness acknowledges that we have been wronged
but it goes beyond that and extends mercy.

Sometimes forgiveness is a process. If we have
been deeply hurt, it takes time for the wound to heal.
In this case forgiveness acts as a continual cleansing

of the wound so that it can heal properly. As we think about a person who has hurt us or sinned against us, feelings of resentment and emotional pain well up. Then we must reaffirm our commitment to forgive them. It is not that the first act of forgiveness was invalid, but that an ongoing process may be necessary until we are completely healed.

I was deeply hurt once by a friend. I could not get over the anger and disappointment I felt every time I thought of him. Another friend advised me that I should tell the Lord I forgave the friend each time these feelings surfaced and say, "Lord, I choose to do this with your love, and I will not give up until you put love in my heart for him. I receive that love by faith."

I prayed that prayer many times a day for months, but nothing seemed to change. Then one day as I prayed, something finally happened—I began to see my friend through new eyes. I saw *his* wounds and hurts; I saw how he had been hurt by his father, and how he was passing those hurts on to me. The Lord released compassion into my heart for him, something I thought would never happen. The Lord did more than I could ask or think!

Move towards people, not away from them

When someone irritates us, or his personality rubs us the wrong way, we tend to avoid him. When he comes into a room, we avoid looking in his direction and move to the other side of the room. Some of us go so far as to steer clear of events or gatherings if certain people will be there.

One of the greatest keys in loving our

adversaries is to move toward them, not away from them. This goes against human nature, but it is effective. We may need time to pray through a difficult relationship, or to cool off after an argument. But we must make the commitment toward the person and work the situation through.

My wife and I sometimes get annoyed with each other, or even have a major disagreement over an issue. When we were first married, we found this an unnerving experience, but it doesn't worry us so much now because we are more secure in our relationship. We have agreed that when this happens, we will take a few hours, or days if need be, to calm down and gain a clearer perspective. Only then will we talk about the issue. We will keep talking about it until we have reached a mutual understanding. It is this mutual commitment to move toward and not away from each other that helps us work through hard times.

What about the person who does not understand these principles and does not want to open up and talk things over? Do all you can to reach out to that person and try to create an atmosphere where he feels he can communicate with you. Most people do want to talk, but don't know how to open up. Meet with him on neutral ground, perhaps over a meal or a cup of coffee, or something he likes to do. Show him you're open, you want things to be right, and you're approachable. When the tension has lessened, you can broach the sensitive areas in your relationship, perhaps asking him if you have done something to hurt him, or if he would be willing to talk about the tension in your relationship.

Don't take up a reproach towards your neighbor

That is good old-fashioned biblical language, meaning we should not receive criticism or a negative report of another person. Don't allow other people's enemies to become yours.

Several years ago, while speaking at a Christian conference, a certain young lady was assigned to be my hostess. She did a superb job, but I found her very irritating and felt critical and uncommunicative toward her. I prayed for her, blessed her, and applied every principle I could think of to overcome my bad attitude, but to no avail.

Finally, on the last day of the conference as I prayed about the situation, the Lord reminded me of a conversation I'd had with someone many months before. They had told me some negative things about my hostess—things I thought I had forgotten. They had lodged deep in my mind and were now affecting my attitude to her. Without knowing it, I had taken up a reproach against someone who had done absolutely nothing against me but had actually bent over backwards to bless me. Realizing what I had done I repented, and those negative feelings left immediately.

What is the correct response to someone who tells us critical and negative things about others? Either stop the conversation and offer to bring the people together for reconciliation, or offer to pray right then for God's answer to the situation. What we must not do is passively receive what is being said; otherwise our minds will quickly become the dumping-ground for other people's rubbish, and we will find ourselves entangled in all kinds of complex, tense relationships.

But what if he is speaking the truth? Spiritually, you don't have to tell lies to slander a person! The point is not whether their statement his true, but whether you should receive a reproach against your neighbor. The only time it is right to discuss someone's faults is when we are involved in a pastoral or counseling relationship with them where discussion aids the process.

While in South Africa several years ago, I met a black Christian. He had been arrested by police sometime before on the suspicion that he was with the African National Congress (a group fighting against the South African government). For several months he was questioned and tortured as the police tried to force a confession from him. However, he had done nothing wrong. Finally he was dumped in the street outside a hospital, nearly dead.

A friend of mine investigated this matter and found to his horror that the policeman in charge of the team "questioning" the black Christian was also a believer. This man had actually helped to beat and torture a brother in Christ, with no firm evidence whatsoever, just hearsay. I prayed with this black Christian in his home. He sobbed deeply as he relived the pain and inhumanity of the situation, but then he chose to forgive his white brother.

While this forgiving love runs contrary to human nature, it is completely consistent with the character of God. This is the superhuman love that shows we have the Holy Spirit living in us. The Bible puts it this way, "The fruit of the Spirit is love, joy, peace, patience, kindness, goodness, faithfulness, gentleness and self-control" (Galatians 5:22). We cannot manufacture these qualities ourselves—we must allow the Holy Spirit to take an active role in our lives if we want to have His fruit.

The list reads very differently when we follow our own way. Paul says, "The acts of the sinful nature are obvious." Among them he names hatred, discord, jealousy, fits of rage, selfish ambition, dissensions, factions and envy, and comments, "Those who live like this will not inherit the kingdom of God" (Galatians 5:19-21). Did you notice how many of the "fruits of the flesh" are related to disunity? We cannot expect to attain either love or unity in the Body of Christ through our own strength. Neither can we expect our lives to draw others into the Kingdom unless we are indwelt by the One who produces the "fruit of the Spirit."

Chapter 6

When Love Seems Impossible

Shortly before the Russian invasion of Czechoslovakia in 1968, a church just outside Prague experienced a terrible schism. Five elders fought it out, but none of them won. Consequently the flock scattered in several directions. Realizing the devastating effect of their behavior, the elders became ashamed of their actions, but were too proud to reach out to one another.

After some time of praying things through, one of the elders took the initiative, went to the others, and admitted his wrong. A spirit of contrition moved through the various factions in the church, and eventually unity and fellowship were restored. Several weeks after this, Russian tanks rolled into the country. Religious and cultural freedom ended abruptly as the new government cracked down hard.

Soon all five elders were arrested. The authorities decided to make them a public example of the consequences of being too vocal about religious matters. A high-ranking officer of the secret police was to interrogate them. Confident that he could get them to incriminate each other, he separated them and began to try to undermine their trust in one another.

To his amazement it did not work. Every time he tried to use half-truths and innuendos from the past to divide them, each would simply reply, "I don't believe my brother would say that about me, and even if he did, I forgive him!"

Eventually the officer became so frustrated with this unusual response that he called all five of the men into his office and demanded to know why they loved each other so much. It wasn't long before he was on his knees, asking God to fill him with the same love.

This story inspires and encourages me because it shows five men who really failed in the area of unity and commitment, and yet were prepared to repent and forgive each other. As a result, a strong bond was formed between them that was a powerful testimony to other people, withstanding even professional interrogation.

They had learned from their mistakes. So, too, must we. In this chapter I want to look at some of the major causes of disunity among Christians.

Jealousy is an insidious attitude that creeps into our hearts when we take our eyes off God and put them onto others. We can be jealous of another's gifts or position in a church or group, or of the high spiritual profile of another's ministry. The Bible says that measuring ourselves against each other is not wise (2 Corinthians 10:12).

We must constantly be on guard against jealousy in our lives, because it can easily take us unawares. I hadn't considered myself a jealous person until last year when I found I was comparing myself rather a lot with a friend. I began wishing I had the same ministry he had. When I recognized this as jealousy I repented. But it reminded me that we never become immune to Satan's tactics as he tries to render us ineffective and rob us of the joy of serving God.

Ambitious and insecure people are particularly susceptible to jealousy. It is not a sin to be ambitious, as long as our motives are pure and we long to give God glory. By prayerfully going through the following checklist, we can discover if we need God to help us in this area. As Christians we must examine our hearts for signs of jealousy, and if we find any, confess them and ask God to renew our minds.

- Jealous people are driven; they feel a great pressure to prove themselves and catch up with others.

- They constantly compare themselves with others.

- They do not rejoice with others when they are promoted or receive recognition.

- They are reluctant to promote anything that does not benefit them directly.

- They fear being overlooked by people, rather than looking to God for affirmation.

- They are hostile and angry towards those of whom they are jealous.

- They mistrust those of whom they are jealous. They convince themselves that they deserve what the other person has, and that the other person has manipulated them out of it.

- They are unable to promote others for fear they might be outshined.

- They secretly rejoice when others fail.

Pride

Pride works like acid, slowly eroding all that is good. Some sin is quite obvious, but pride is subtle and deceptive: "The pride of your heart has deceived you" (Obadiah 3).

By examining the fruit of pride, we can discover its presence in our life. Pride produces arrogance and a blind self-righteousness. That is to say, the proud one cannot see his arrogance — those around him can! A proud person is unteachable; he finds it hard to receive correction, and rarely, if ever, admits he is wrong.

In the Body of Christ, people are separated from each other not so much because they have sinned, but because they are too proud to admit that they have sinned. We are not divided because of "theological disagreement," but because we are too proud to learn from one another.

Success and blessing often lead to the deadly practice of self-congratulation. We regard ourselves as the very chosen of God, and point to our success as proof that we are special objects of His divine favor. Thus, anyone who dares to correct us must be wrong. Or, if they have something to say, we can't listen to it until they get their "critical attitude" right.

It is easier to listen and respond if someone comes to offer criticism in the right way. But even if they don't have the right attitude, we should have the humility to listen to them and consider their hurts and grievances.

May God give us grace to heed this warning against pride. I have found the prayer below helpful in exposing this area of my life to the light of the Holy Spirit:

Dear heavenly Father,

Help me to receive correction from any person, friend or enemy. Lord, it has been a long time since I have admitted my sins and been willing to be corrected. Enable me to accept the fact that I need others to help me see my sins and weaknesses. When people point out a wrong, I will pray about it; and the more offended I am, the more I will pray.

I need to learn from others in Your Body, Lord—especially those with whom I disagree. I choose to commit myself to building unity between various groups in the Body of Christ, particularly those I have looked down on in the past. I am willing to use my time to serve these other groups.

Forgive me for my pride, Father. I choose, by Your grace, to walk in humility. I understand that this means I am willing for others to know who I really am, including my weaknesses

and sin. I want to be teachable; I want
to esteem those whom I once considered weak. I want to be identified
with those parts of the Body of Christ
that I have despised.

Help me to be more concerned
about what You require me to do next,
rather than what I have achieved for
You in the past. I am an unworthy servant and I don't deserve praise nor
recognition. I will seek to promote
those who ignore me, and bless others
rather than seek recognition for myself.

Thank You for Your forgiveness—in
Jesus' name. Amen.

Independence

Independence is another great barrier to unity. Basi-
cally it is a selfish attitude that expresses itself in the
determination to "do it my way." Independent people
are more concerned with what they want than what
others need. They are stubborn and inflexible, run-
ning from church to church looking for one with
which they can agree entirely on every point.

Independent people do not really care much
about unity because they are consumed with the
desire for things to be done their own way. They rebel
against spiritual leaders because they do not want to
be in submission to anyone. They excuse themselves
by talking about the priesthood of all believers, or
accusing leaders of being authoritarian. Independence is a great curse on spiritual unity.

Hardness of heart

Another great hindrance to unity is the hardness of people's hearts and their consequent refusal to make restitution when they have wronged others. The Bible teaches that if we sin against someone we must not only ask God's forgiveness, we should go to the one we have hurt and ask his forgiveness (Matthew 5:23-24).

When we are in a right relationship with God, we will want to be in a right relationship with others. We will have a tenderness of heart which some call "brokenness." If I have sinned against someone, or even hurt him inadvertently, unity can be maintained by going to him and making things right.

If I allow barriers to go up between us, even if the other person was mostly at fault, I have sinned. God holds us accountable to go to others: "Therefore, if you are offering your gift at the altar and there remember that your brother has something against you, leave your gift there in front of the altar. First go and be reconciled to your brother; then come and offer your gift" (Matthew 5:23-24).

Many excuses spring to mind to prevent us from doing this. "It was such a little thing—surely it doesn't matter now?" Or, "People won't respect me if I tell them what I did." And, "Surely God doesn't want to embarrass me, does He?" Or even, "God has forgiven me. I don't have to uncover something that is under the blood of Jesus." If I have approached the person and he refuses to discuss the matter, I may rationalize, "The ball's in his court now. It's his problem, not mine."

Each of these excuses reflects either hardness of

heart, or ignorance of biblical teaching on restitution. Our sins are definitely under the blood of Jesus when we repent and ask His forgiveness. But the fruit of true repentance is making things right with those we have sinned against, as well as with the Lord Jesus. The Bible teaches that when a person truly repents, he will restore what is stolen and apologize to those whom he has hurt (Matthew 3:8; Acts 26:20).

We are to go to people and ask for forgiveness when we have wronged them. We must be willing to die to our reputation, and be more concerned about what Jesus thinks than others' opinions. People usually respect humility and openness. Although a long struggle may be involved in seeking forgiveness, it is always worthwhile.

Busyness

Busyness is a subtle but deadly deterrent to unity. So far we have looked at sins that prevent unity, but did you realize that busyness can also effectively block unity? Unity is built on relationships, not roles, and it takes time to build relationships. We can be busy serving the Lord, but still not be building love and unity. Why? Because God is interested in much more than full diaries and great outreaches. He wants more, much more, than church buildings filled with people on Sundays.

Unity can wilt and die; it must be cultivated by prayer and watered by times of fellowship. If you're a person with lots of ideas, you will be tempted to instigate unity prayer cells, unity rallies, and unity conferences. But perhaps the greatest thing you can do to build unity is to step back, and patiently allow unity to grow by cultivating deep and long-lasting relationships.

A few years ago, some of the men in our mission in Amsterdam were having a meal together. Talking around the meal table, we discovered that all of us were experiencing the same feelings of frustration about the superficial level of our friendships and fellowship. After some prayer, we committed ourselves to a new level of openness in our relationships.

We were all very excited about it, and I immediately wanted to call meetings with our staff workers and tell them about our commitment. Fortunately, someone in the group was wise enough to suggest that perhaps we should be canceling meetings for our staff, not adding more.

We did just that. We slowed the work schedule down and prayed that what God had done in our hearts would be repeated in the hearts of our fellow workers. And it was! People began to notice that we were spending more time together, and they too began to pray together more and enjoy more relaxed times of fellowship. Since that time there has been a marked change in our community.

It is essential that we establish our priorities in order to release the time needed to build strong relationships that make for unity. We need to ask God to reveal His plan and show us those things He would have us sacrifice in order to develop relationships with others. People must be more important to us than our programs; quality must take priority over quantity, and our families must come before other people.

A year ago, Sally and I found ourselves beginning to resent the work in which we were involved—somehow the joy had gone out of it. We felt we had lost control of own lives and that schedules were controlling us rather than the reverse. We lived and worked in the same building and were unable to get away from the constant demands upon us.

Consequently, we set about making some changes in how we made decisions, and took some practical steps to keep our home-life separate from our work. We started planning our time off so that the family would not be squeezed out. We prayed, asking the Lord to restore us in this area of our lives. Prayer, planning, practical steps, and a refreshing holiday did the trick. Now we enjoy our work more than ever. Not only do we have enough time for those we want to be with, but we seem to achieve more as well.

Is it time for you to evaluate your priorities and bring some things under control?

Chapter 7

Tough Love

Real love desires the best for others. Real love is not only tender, it must also be tough. We must be tough in our convictions, but tender in how we express them to others. This means getting involved with difficult people, confronting those who hurt us, and standing up to those who try to use us. It involves gently disciplining those who fall into sin, and expecting a greater level of accountability among our fellow brothers and sisters in Christ. The word *church* loses credibility when we are unwilling to get involved in one another's lives and hold each other accountable for attitudes and actions. It is difficult to find the right balance between toughness and tenderness, and we often learn the hard way.

Robert, overwhelmed by depression, insecurity and fear, came to us for help. Every time we caught sight of the slash marks across his wrists, it reminded us of the seriousness of his situation. If we were not careful, we could have a suicide on our hands. What we didn't realize was that Robert wanted us to think exactly that. At first he fitted in well. But as time went on more and more of our energy and planning began to revolve around his wants and needs. If things did not go his way, he began throwing temper tantrums, hurling allegations that we didn't really want to help him, and threatening suicide. On several occasions he even attempted it.

The responsibility of having him under our care weighed heavily upon us. It drained us of our joy and sense of community. Finally I realized that something had to be done about the situation, but I wasn't sure what. One thing was for certain, though—I didn't want his blood on my hands!

Fortunately, a friend and Bible teacher came to visit and helped us resolve the situation. He pointed out that we were allowing ourselves to be manipulated, and that the ultimate goal of our ministry was not to keep Robert happy at any cost. We, in fact, were not loving him by allowing him to walk all over us.

The confusion lifted. I could see that in the guise of love we were really rewarding and reinforcing his immature, manipulative behavior. It had to be challenged. I told him that we loved him and would do anything within reason to see him healed and helped, but we would do so on a different basis in the future. I explained that from now on he could only stay and receive help for his problems on the terms we set out. If he took his life, that was his responsibility, not ours—he was the one who would have to answer to God. If he wanted help, and if we saw openness in his attitude and a willingness to grow spiritually, we would help him work through his problems.

At first it was hard for Robert, and also for some of our friends who were motivated by mercy. However as we studied God's word together, we saw that love involves holiness as well as mercy and compassion. Real love means standing firm on God's principles of holiness. Such commitment is hard to find in today's world where tolerance, open-mindedness and doing your own thing are all important — even to the extent of sacrificing integrity. Quick solutions may be attractive, but they are often superficial.

Many people have the same manipulative, demanding attitude as Robert. We may meet them at work, or in our neighborhood, sports club, or church. In the church, manipulation destroys love and unity. We must learn to recognize it and confront it head on, whether it is in the intimate relationship of our marriage, or in our wider relationships.

Manipulation is any attempt to control, obligate, use or take advantage of others by dishonest or unfair means. Insecure people use it to bolster themselves in the eyes of others. Frustrated or proud people use it to control others, or maneuver things to their advantage, while power-hungry people seize on it to get to the top. Impatient people are often manipulative, believing that results are more important than the people they step over along the way.

Manipulation may be blatant or subtle, relying on calculated hints, preconceived facial expressions, and careful scheming. For some it is an ingrained, subconscious habit-pattern, while others revert to it only when under pressure.

The pity manipulator

This person seeks to gain sympathy through appearing to be weak, needy, or misunderstood. He uses sickness, depression, threats, and anything else that will get people feeling sorry for him. He often comes across as the wounded victim, using hurts of the past to demand help. Such a person appears to be very weak until you cross his will — then he explodes in an eruption of anger. Robert frequently resorted to this type of behavior. He enjoyed keeping everyone in suspense as to what he was going to do next.

Initially our response to Robert actually reinforced his manipulative behavior. However, once we recognized it for what it was, we were able to challenge him and deal with the problem. We could have allowed it to continue, and deceived ourselves that our response was one of true Christian love. However, the most loving response in this type of situation is to confront. Robert had to be confronted with his behavior and see it for what it was. Only then could we begin to deal with it.

The power manipulator

This person uses sheer strength of personality to flatten his opposition. He fits in well socially if things are going his way, but becomes dogmatic and domineering when they're not. He is often totally oblivious to how he has pushed others into submission.

Such a person is convinced that he knows what is best, and so he tends not to listen and rarely apologizes. He enjoys correcting others and pointing out their faults, often making snide remarks or using caustic humor in the process.

"Spiritual" power manipulators play on the fact that people are very reluctant to contradict God, so they claim to have special guidance from Him. What do you say when someone announces that the Lord has authorized him to do something that doesn't complement the overall vision of the group or church? Difficult and divisive problems can ensue. Some try to use their spiritual gifts to coerce people into submitting to them or doing unpleasant tasks that they want to avoid.

I Samuel 15:23 (RSV) says, "Stubbornness is as iniquity and idolatry." This could well refer to those who use their spiritual gifts to control others. In the context of this passage, Saul had used his spiritual gifts to rally a nation to disobedience, but when questioned by Samuel, he quickly blamed those under him for instigating the disobedience. The verse quoted above is part of Samuel's reply.

A clear mark of a spiritually manipulative person is the intimidation of others to the point where they feel embarrassed or frightened to challenge the other's stand. For the sake of the Body of Christ, these people must be challenged and brought to accountability for their manipulative influence over others.

Power manipulators may use anger to control others. After all, who wants to be continually met with a storm of anger and ensuing tension when they make a suggestion? It's much easier to give in, and people normally do. Sadly, they often think that to back down is the only "Christian" response to the problem.

The "I want to serve you" manipulator

Have you ever had someone ask how you are, only to
find that person using your honest answer to analyze
your problems, or lay hands on you and pray over
you? He is, in fact, encroaching into your life without
invitation and with dubious motives. He may be offering to serve you in order to create an obligation or
sense of dependency that will make you feel indebted
to him in an unhealthy way. He worms his way into
situations that bring him close to spiritual leaders or
those in positions of authority. Once there, he hides
behind the spiritual facade of wanting to be a servant
in order to get what he wants.

John arrived at a time when we were snowed
under with work, and offered to ease the load in any
way he could. He insisted that he was there to serve
us and our ministry. The first couple of weeks were
great—he ran errands for us and helped in the office.
As we got to know him better, he asked if I could
spare some time for counseling him. I agreed, despite
my full schedule—after all, he was such a help to us.

By the end of the first month, I caught myself
telling Sally that we really ought to be doing this or
that for John and wondering if he was happy, or if I
was spending enough time with him. It was then that
it dawned on me how crazy the situation had
become—initially John had come insisting on serving
us, but now he was taking more of our time than he
was saving. It wasn't that we didn't want to help John,
but he had not been honest with us. He had
manipulated us by rationalizing, "I'm doing this for
you, so you have to do this for me."

It's easy to use this form of manipulation in

marriage. Under the guise of "honoring" our partner, we can manipulate them to get what we really want. I might want a new jacket, but instead of openly discussing the need, I offer to take my wife shopping and buy her a new dress. After I've encouraged her to spend by saying how much I love her and want her to have the best, we just happen to spot "my" jacket. Because she has a new dress she feels cornered into agreeing to my buying the jacket. Instead of me going home feeling special, she feels manipulated and used.

The information manipulator

Information is power, as the saying goes, and withholding information in certain situations can have a great influence on the outcome. We have all experienced the feeling of injustice that occurs when someone gives a report about us that is incomplete or twisted in order to color other people's view of a situation. It is technically possible to tell the truth about a person or situation and yet not be truthful. The pledge to "tell the truth, the whole truth, and nothing but the truth" must have been written by someone who understood human nature well! How easy it is to slant an issue our way by being selective in the parts of the truth we share. Such selectivity is a million miles from the very proper desire not to destroy someone with "total honesty" (see page 50).

Some people love to extract information from us about situations or people, and then use it out of context either to back us into a corner or rally others around their cause. There is nothing worse than hearing something that you said in good faith come back to you in this destructive way.

We may be probed as to how we feel about someone, which plants seeds of doubt about them in our mind. Sometimes information is imparted to shade conversations or relationships to the person's advantage, while others may withhold information to maintain control of positions, relationships, or jobs.

As these various forms of manipulation have been identified, you may be aware of some of the traits in your own life. If so, don't be discouraged—the first step in growing out of manipulative behavior is to recognize it. Ask your heavenly Father to help you to honestly assess your weaknesses, and allow the light of the Holy Spirit to reveal motives to you. Repent of the way you have used others to your own end, and ask those whom you have hurt to forgive you. To prevent the pattern from recurring, especially if it is an ingrained one, seek the safeguard of godly men and women who will commit themselves to discipling you in this area. Confess the problem to the people who are most affected by your behavior. Finally, meditate on Scriptures about pure motives, "Blessed are the pure in heart, for they will see God" (Matthew 5:8). Cultivate childlike simplicity in your thoughts and behavior and refuse to adopt manipulative attitudes towards others.

If you are a parent, you will recognize some, if not all of this behavior in your children. Manipulation begins very early on. Just watch a four-year-old who doesn't want to eat his dinner—the faces he pulls, the sick stomach, the big crocodile tears, the remonstrations of, "If you loved me you wouldn't make me eat this," or, "Tom's mother doesn't make him eat peas." They're all brilliant manipulative tactics. What about when it's bedtime and Susie has a sudden urge to help with the dishes or do extra homework? We are not doing our children any favors by ignoring such behavior. We are to bring our children up from an early age to live in a godly way (Proverbs 22:6). If we allow our children to establish manipulative behavior by rewarding it, or not confronting them with it, we do them a great injustice for which they will not thank us later.

The wider Body of Christ must also be open to challenge those who manipulate. It's tough love in action that is needed, not taking the easy way out. How do we go about this? Firstly, we must choose to forgive others for the influence they have tried to exert over us. We must also closely watch our motives and reactions—it's so easy to lash back using the same tactics. We must resist and respond in the opposite spirit. Remember, those doing the manipulating have more often than not been the victim of manipulation themselves, so don't let the cycle perpetuate itself through you.

If we suspect that we're being manipulated, we should get to the bottom of the situation for the sake of everyone involved. There are many appropriate ways to do this. It may simply mean finding out both sides of a story to make sure we have the whole truth. It may entail standing our ground on an issue rather than taking the path of least resistance. If the manipulation is serious, the best course of action may be to share what has happened with a pastor or church leader and allow him to deal with the situation. Whatever the case, if the manipulation goes unchecked it will breed mistrust and suspicion, making people wary of each other and stifling open communication through fear of being misinterpreted.

Make decisions that are based on principles and not pressure. This is particularly hard if you are an indecisive or insecure person. You may need to talk things through with a friend and determine how you are going to act on certain issues. If you're taken off guard, don't make a rash, binding decision. Allow time to distance yourself from the immediate problem, whenever possible, and think things through—pray, and seek counsel if necessary. If you have to take the responsibility for a decision, make sure that you feel it is the right one.

If striving and competition are tolerated, then encouragement, appreciation of others, and serving and honoring one another is relegated to the back benches while criticism and factions take over. Manipulation, if left unchecked, is a sure way to demolish unity.

Manipulation through Christian media

Unfortunately, there are those in the Christian media who use their position to manipulate unwary believers. The same television show, book, or radio station that brings us the Gospel can also expose Christianity's "dirty laundry." Some high-profile Christians have assumed the role of "watchdog of the faith," publicly denouncing believers with whom they disagree. They use their platform in the media to stir us into disunity with those we don't even know. By using selective pieces of the truth, the power of their personality, and the guise that they are "serving us" by making us aware of error, they bring shame to

Christ's name and ruin to His servants. They believe
their God-given ministry is to make the Church aware
of dangerous doctrines and unbiblical trends, and in
so doing they publicly hurt and humiliate those they
feel are in error. They attract wounded, disillusioned
followers who love to hear things that will feed their
own bitterness and prejudices.

God will hold us accountable for every idle and
judgmental word we speak, and Scripture underlines
the dangers of a divisive, argumentative person as
much as it does those with doctrinal inconsistencies.
In Ephesians 4:29-32, Paul tells us to speak only that
which will help and build up the listener. To plant
seeds of doubt about the integrity of others in the
Body of Christ is equated with attacking the Lord
Jesus Himself (I Corinthians 3:16-19), and Galatians
5:15 warns, "If you keep on biting and devouring each
other, watch out or you will be destroyed by each
other."

There is a tremendous difference between a
warning concerning doctrinal extremism and actually
calling people heretics by name, or worse still,
inferring that some people are dabbling in the realm
of the occult because they do something with which
we disagree, or because they describe their beliefs in
terms unfamiliar to us. Obviously, doctrine must be
biblical, but great caution needs to be exercised in
labeling individuals heretics or false prophets.

The Bible makes it clear that we are not to
engage ourselves in correcting another person's
problems unless we are personally and redemptively
involved with him. Unless the person is a proven false
prophet or a dangerous deceiver, then accusations
should not be made publicly against him. Although

we should discuss ideas and doctrines, we must avoid judging individuals.

Tough love is not another name for ripping to shreds anyone with whom we disagree. It is tragic to see what is done in the name of loving our brother. I have seen books that destroy other Christians' credibility and cast doubt and suspicion on various groups. There they are, for sale in window displays—displays whose purpose is supposedly evangelistic. If a non-Christian were to buy one, what would he think? Would it draw him closer to the truth, or would it completely alienate? Before we bring "family" business into the public arena, we need to ask some serious questions about our motivation and the effect it will have on all concerned.

The church does not need prophets who speak with harshness and lack of concern for those they attack. The Old Testament prophets who called others to repentance did so in brokenness and humility, often weeping over the sin they were confronting. They openly identified with those God had sent them to warn, rather than setting themselves above them and leveling accusations against them—an attitude that is all too prevalent today. We need brokenhearted prophets—men and women who have heard from God and will call His church to holiness and love for one another.

Let us stand together in true love and unity as Christian brothers and sisters demonstrating to the world the presence and power of Christ. Let us turn away from the manipulation of information and the judgmental attitudes that so often cast a slur across the whole Body of Christ. Instead, may each of us determine to strive for unity and not divisiveness, and may those who feel God has called them to correct others in the public arena do so in brokenness and humility.

Chapter 8

Where the Decisions Are Made

Nothing brings out the fallen nature of man like a full-blown church quarrel. Annual business meetings, board meetings, and leaders' gatherings often appear to give as much opportunity to the devil as they do to God. The principles of love, acceptance and unity are jettisoned, and the meeting turns into a free-for-all. People arrive bristling with statistics and other details necessary to support their positions, or, with a self-proclaimed monopoly on the will of God for the situation, which is used as an excuse for not listening to and respecting the opinions of others.

In the typical Christian meeting where a decision has to be reached, one of the following four approaches is often employed.

1. The competitive approach

Here politics take over, and anything is employed that helps achieve the aim of getting an idea passed.

Manipulation, pressure tactics, and back room maneuvering may all be used. Prayer is a formality, and any suggestion that God may want to speak directly to His people about the decision is greeted with unbelief.

2. The conflictive approach

In this approach, strong personalities dominate. Issues are seen as black-and-white, and decision-making becomes an "either/or" proposition. There is no middle ground — either I'm totally right and you're wrong, or vice versa. This frequently results in an emotionally charged atmosphere where pride and stubbornness predominate. In these situations, where the most persuasive element "wins" and everyone else "loses," more heat than light is generated. Prayer is taken seriously, but all too often it is prayer that others will see the issues "my way."

3. The constructive approach

This is where committees of mature, levelheaded men — and sometimes a token woman — carefully construct the will of God by common sense, good business principles, and "gentlemanly fair play."

Much can be said for this approach to decision-making, but its inherent weakness is the tendency to rely heavily on human wisdom and resources in arriving at the best plan. Prayer is merely seeking God's seal of approval on the decision already made; not involving Him in the process. Intellect can easily rule supreme, even over the voice of the Holy Spirit.

4. The cop-out approach

I coined this term after watching those who are so spiritual that they cop out on reality. They push all the responsibility onto God, and become so "heavenly-minded" that they are of no earthly use.

They certainly believe in prayer. They have usually already prayed and received the "right" answer, so they feel no need to listen to others. Unfortunately, they have forgotten that the Bible tells us to love God with our minds, which doesn't mean that "we hang them up with our coats and hats when we come to church," as one pastor told me, adding, "We come here to worship God, not think."

Whenever a decision has to be made which affects those in a group or church, there is potential for hurt, anger, bitterness, mistrust, and a breakdown of unity. Aware of this, I have increasingly appreciated the importance of balance. In our decision-making we need a combination of acknowledging the sovereignty of God, listening diligently to hear His voice, searching the Bible to discover what He has already said, seeking the counsel of godly men and women, and thinking through the practical implications of a decision.

I call this the *cooperative approach.* It is grounded in the belief that people are more important than programs; that maintaining unity is as important to God as the decision itself, and that "when brothers live together in unity . . . there the Lord bestows his blessing" (Psalm 133).

Paul emphasizes the importance of unity in I Corinthians 1:10, "I appeal to you, brothers, in the name of our Lord Jesus Christ, that all of you agree with one another so that there may be no divisions among you and that you may be perfectly united in mind and thought."

Paul is not suggesting that we agree with each other over particular issues, but that we should have a spirit of agreement that transcends all our disagreements.

If we are to be of one mind, we must have one heart. However, having the mind of Christ (Philippians 2:5) does not necessarily mean having the right answer, but rather the right attitude. It means laying down our rights, being a servant to the vision and needs of others, and honoring others above ourselves. Without a Christlike attitude, particularly towards those with whom we disagree, we cannot reach a decision acceptable to God.

The essence of the cooperative approach

1. Commitment to one another

In Acts 15:1-5 there is a conflict. Brothers have come to Antioch from Jerusalem saying that Gentiles cannot become Christians unless they obey the Jewish law. Naturally, the church in Antioch, which is not Jewish, is very upset. However, they do not throw out the messengers and decide to continue on as an independent, disconnected group. Instead they take positive steps to try and resolve the situation.

They are committed to the church in Jerusalem, and so they send Paul and Barnabas there in an attempt to resolve the tension. Instead of withdrawing themselves when faced with this intrusion into their church life, they move closer to their brothers in Jerusalem. They are committed to working through and finding an answer to the conflict.

Human tendency, when we're hurt or disagree with people, is to withdraw and break off fellowship. But these believers were so committed to each other that, even when faced with a sharp disagreement, they would not give up, lose hope, become bitter and judgmental, or withdraw. When we are faced with disagreements, we also must go to our brothers and sisters in openness, love, and a forgiving attitude, and work the situation through.

2. Responsible leadership

In Antioch, the church leaders accepted the responsibility for resolving the conflict (Acts 15:6). We must accept authority if there is to be unity in the church, and especially unity in the area of decision-making.

The spiritual leadership of a group or church has the final responsibility, before God, for decisions made and the direction and life of the church. Scripture clearly indicates that there must be spiritual authority (Acts 20:28; I Thessalonians 5:12; II Timothy 2:24-25; 4:2; Titus 1:5-7; I Peter 5:1-5; Hebrews 13:17), and that that authority is responsible for guiding and governing the Body of Christ.

That authority, though, should not be seen in terms of position but relationship. In other words, true spiritual authority is the sum total of what a person is in Christ—maturity, experience, wisdom, character, motivation, obedience to the Word, and gifting, and does not reside in a particular position or title. If a person has to call upon his title or position to give him his authority, then he has, in fact, lost it.

Spiritual authority should not be viewed as an exclusive responsibility or right, giving a leader the prerogative to tell people what they should or should not do in their personal lives. Of course, leaders should be concerned about people's personal welfare, and love them enough to confront them where there is sin. But it is the responsibility of the individual to make decisions in his own life, even if the leadership feels they are the wrong choices.

Biblical authority is rooted in relationship. It is characterized by trust, love, and servanthood. When relationships break down, for whatever reason, authority is lost. To force an issue at that point is to employ fleshly power, not spiritual authority. Authority is offered, not seized. It is leading by serving, not pushing by manipulation and heavy-handed control.

Wise and responsible leaders will be pioneers, pointing out the direction in which to go, and also in contact with the members of the body, including them in making major decisions. James had a position of authority in the church at Jerusalem, but he chose to involve the whole church in the decision-making process (Acts 15:13-22).

When a leader does not lead, or when people are not trusted and included in the decision-making process, an imbalance occurs that upsets the whole spiritual equilibrium of a church. A wise leader must be in front, pointing in the direction to go; but not so far in front that he loses contact with the people. Neither of these extremes is right—the leader must not simply give orders; nor should the congregation rule through the vote.

3. Right relationships

If there is to be unity in decision-making, then all those involved should be in right relationship with one another. Unresolved conflicts and hurts, and lack of brokenness or repentance over wounds caused to others, all raise walls and, more importantly, grieve the Holy Spirit.

We may make excuses for not going to others when there are personality conflicts, but the Holy Spirit does not accept conflicts between believers. Personality differences, yes, but conflicts, no.

It is tempting to live with these "natural" conflicts by avoiding one another, and ignoring the promptings of the Holy Spirit to go work them through. We often blame others for the conflict, dismissing any responsibility to go and make it right. But it takes two to have a conflict.

The fact that there is conflict points to a need for spiritual growth. Realizing this will help us accept conflicts as opportunities to deal with areas of weakness in our own character and thus to become more Christlike. There is no conflict from which we cannot learn when we accept this responsibility and work through our differences. Do we really expect God to be guiding us as a group if we are not honoring Him in our relationships?

4. Singleness of vision

It is absolutely essential to have one clear vision as a group. As Amos 3:3 says, "Do two walk together unless they have agreed to do so?" There must be a clear understanding of the basic direction and operating principles of a group or church. Without this it will flounder. Absence of clear vision from the Lord and its declaration by leadership create a vacuum that many will be tempted to fill.

5. *Submissiveness of heart*

We need to have a submissive heart that will support any decision the group makes, so long as it is not unethical or immoral. After submitting our convictions about a matter, we must trust God that He will guide the leaders and group to the right decision. It is possible to disagree and still have unity, because unity is a matter of heart attitude and not absolute agreement.

Decision-making in unity happens when there is a common understanding of God's will. When there is disagreement over what is God's will in a situation, the leaders of the group should call the people to further prayer. They should ask God to give the group new perspective to clarify His will.

This can only be done when each person believes that God, in His wisdom, will not give any one person the complete understanding of what is right. Each person needs the contribution of others in the group to know God's will.

People are sometimes wrong, of course, and that is why there must be submissiveness of heart to the Lord and to one another.

6. *Good communication*

Our first priority is to have good communication with the Lord. Many of us are not adequately prepared for a "spiritually rewarding discussion" until we have had time to pray. How many times have you reacted adversely to a proposal, only to find that you have a completely different perspective on it after prayer and reflection?

Prayer allows us to die to our own thoughts and desires. It gives us time to read the Word and seek God for His perspective on a matter. It also allows Him to show us His burden in the situation. We often become prematurely involved in a decision because we have not allowed God to touch our hearts with His love and compassion for those people affected by that decision. Softness of heart often brings an entirely different perspective on a situation.

We should also cultivate good communication with each other. This must include teaching on how to make important decisions together according to biblical principles. Once members of the group have agreed on the basic principles regarding the decision-making process, they will support that process more fully, and understand their part in it. They will think and respond in a more mature way.

Where a few individuals tend to spoil discussion and decision-making through their divisiveness and immaturity, the individuals should be corrected in private. The proper way to participate in corporate decision-making should be explained to them. It may be necessary to ask the divisive members to be silent in discussion times until they can participate in a mature manner. Don't pass rules that restrict the entire group because of a few people.

Leaders need to draw people out and help them communicate. Sometimes the quiet ones have the greatest wisdom, but they may find it difficult to voice their concerns. Take time for people.

Most people want to know that their viewpoint is valued by the group, including the leaders. If they are assured of this, they are much more likely to support the decision that the group makes, even if they disagree with it.

There must also be good communication about the decision that is being made. There is nothing worse than to be pushed into a decision when we do not have adequate information or sufficient time to consider it. People should be given the background to the decision, and any previous guidance should be explained very thoroughly.

We should give time to all those concerned before asking them to make a decision. I often encourage leaders and the more vocal members of a group not to make value judgments, nor give their personal feelings about a decision until adequate time and information have been given to all concerned.

The less vocal people must be allowed to express their feelings without fear of rejection or censure. It's even important to wait for prayer until after the discussion process. Expressing our emotions often paves the way for being able to pray about a decision. Some members of the group may need time to share their concerns and raise their questions privately. They must know that they will be loved and encouraged if they share their deepest anxieties. This kind of openness and acceptance builds trust and assures people that they are more important than the decision itself. It lays the foundation for making a decision in unity, even if there is disagreement. Because unity has to do with an attitude of heart, it is possible to make a decision where everyone does not agree on every aspect or detail, but where there is total unity of heart.

My father has a saying: "You can take two cats, tie their tails together, and hang them over a clothesline; you will have union, but you won't have unity!" Unity does not happen simply because people are thrown together in the same place at the same time. Unity is a work of the Holy Spirit, and we must invite Him to do His work in our hearts. Let us determine not to settle for union in our decisions and relationships, but to listen and obey His leading until we attain unity in the Spirit in the bond of love.

Chapter 9

Leaders Are Human Too

Several people stayed around after the lecture—some had questions, others just wanted to say hello. Among them was a young woman who had a grim expression on her face. "My name is Julia," she began. "I just want you to know that I don't trust you!"

I looked at her closely, trying to understand why she should say such a startling thing. Did she know me from somewhere? Had she listened to some rumor about me? Collecting my thoughts together, I asked, "Did I say something that offended you?"

"No," she replied, "I just felt I had to tell you that I don't trust you." Now I was really puzzled.

What could have compelled her to say such a thing? As I probed further, it became clear that her hostility was not aimed at me personally, but at authority figures generally. I discovered that she had genuine reasons for her mistrust. A domineering pastor had used the principle of submission to authority to overstep his role and interfere with her

personal life. Her childhood concept of authority also
had been colored by a father who disciplined her
harshly in fits of anger. To ensure that she would not
be hurt again by authority figures, she had taken
offensive action. She had made it a habit to confront
spiritual leaders in the way she had confronted me,
using their reactions to justify her own opinion that
leaders are never to be trusted.

Julia, like so many, had valid reasons to doubt
leaders, but her bitterness and resentment could have
been avoided had she acknowledged that leaders are
human beings just like everyone else. Even though
the New Testament epistles teach that those in
authority are to be righteous, mature men, they do
not say that they are to be perfect. If we put leaders
on a pedestal, then sooner or later we will be
disappointed.

What should we do when a leader fails us? Start
circulating a petition for his resignation? Make sure
everyone knows what he has done, or write to the
bishop or the elders before we have the full facts?
Someone has said that the Church is the only army
which stabs its officers in the back, and we've all seen
it happen. We need to view the situation
calmly—leadership problems often get out of
proportion in the heat of the moment. There is a time
to confront an unjust leader, but how far can we go
before we have "touched the Lord's anointed"?
Should we remain silent in the face of a leader's sin
and trust God to deal with him in due course? These
questions need to be addressed if unity is to become a
reality in our group, church, or organization.

What you do when a leader is wrong depends a
great deal on what is meant by "wrong." A stubborn

pastor who won't back down from a personality conflict is wrong in quite a different way from one who is siphoning church funds. There is a qualitative difference between denying the resurrection of Christ, and arguing over speaking in tongues. We must differentiate between those things which trouble us simply because they violate our personal preferences, and those things which violate biblical truth. How we respond to a leader who is wrong is vital to unity. His wrongness does not excuse us from reacting in a godly manner and following biblical principles. Two wrongs don't make a right!

Sadly, some groups have overemphasized the concept of submission to the point where the average church member is afraid of using his common sense or conscience. He is unable to admit, even to himself, that his leader is fallible. Discerning a person's weakness is not sin—patience, forgiveness, and corrective discipline have no meaning unless we are allowed to be aware of one another's faults.

The Bible teaches that God alone is worthy of our total allegiance and absolute obedience. Submission to spiritual leaders must be conditional on our right to uphold scriptural principles. Since submission is an attitude of heart, it is possible to disobey a leader submissively. Conversely, it is possible to obey and yet be rebellious in heart.

Some groups teach that lay people are not spiritual enough to challenge or correct a leader. Pride is at the root of this teaching, and since it is usually leaders that give the teaching, it becomes a way for insecure leaders to avoid accountability. It results in a *Catch 22* situation—only a *spiritual* person can correct a leader, but a spiritual person knows that it is not right to do so. According to this line of reasoning, if you try to correct the leader, you must be in the wrong and no one should listen to you because you're not spiritual. The result: a leader is beyond correction.

The Bible teaches that character, not position or title, is the qualification needed for someone to challenge or correct a leader. Galatians 6:1 says that those who are spiritual should restore those who are caught in sin. Those who correct should be mature and humble. It says nothing about position or title.

We should also be very careful about quoting Scripture at one another in these situations. An overbearing leader will often hide behind verses that are quoted entirely out of context. The writers of the Epistles did not intend their writings to be used as ammunition to be hurled at others. They were written from a distance, addressing various situations that needed correcting.

I don't believe that Paul would have wanted wives to scatter copies of Ephesians 5:25, "Husbands, love your wives, just as Christ loved the church," through their husbands' belongings. Nor did he envisage husbands treating their wives like children, using, "Wives, submit to your husbands as to the Lord" as justification (Ephesians 5:22). If Sally and I were to resort to quoting Scripture accusingly at each other, we would both be focusing on our "rights" and not our responsibilities. Unity would go out the window, and there would be little chance that either of us would change for the better.

The same is true of submission and authority in the Church. The Bible's emphasis for leaders is not on teaching people to submit but on being "shepherds of God's flock that is under your care, serving as overseers—not because you must, but because you are willing, as God wants you to be; not greedy for money, but eager to serve; not lording it over those entrusted to you, but being examples to the flock" (I Peter 5:2-3). Obviously, a leader needs to teach the whole truth on this issue, which includes respect and submission. But he should not twist this element to give himself rights as a leader. Rather, he should focus on his own responsibilities and obligations.

Biblical principles for responding to leaders when they are wrong

The question remains, "What exactly should we do when we feel a leader is wrong?" The following principles will help in answering that question:

1. Check your attitude.

Are you reacting out of hurt, bitterness, or disappointment over something done to you or someone close to you? Are you angry because you thought a "man of God" would never do such a thing? If so, you could well make matters worse by getting involved in the situation. God does not want resentment to infect our spirits, so beware if you find no compassion in your heart for the leader. Remember, "Above all, love each other deeply, because love covers over a multitude of sins" (I Peter 4:8).

God's motive is always to restore those who have fallen—He is our Redeemer. If you have been hurt by someone, then you must choose whether to hold onto it and allow it to destroy your joy, or to keep on forgiving until you get the victory. Each time that person comes to mind, forgive them—even if it is a hundred times a day (see Matthew 18:21-22). God will heal your pain and give you a fresh love for the person.

2. Pray for the leader.

Are you willing to stand in the gap and intercede for the leader? God can use your prayer as an agent for change in his life. Pray for circumstances that will help the person realize the seriousness and the implications of what he has done. Pray with humility, waiting for God to give you a heart of love and mercy towards your leader.

If the issue is not sin but a personality conflict, choose to receive love for him by faith. Ask God what He wants you to learn from the situation, and for a revelation of your heart and motives. How many of us are prepared to pray diligently, or even once, for someone with whom we come into conflict? It is so easy to concentrate on how we can turn the situation to our advantage, or get back at the person. We fill our minds with details of his weaknesses, instead of asking God to strengthen him.

3. Make sure the facts are correct.

The Bible warns us not to judge until we have heard both sides of an issue. "He who answers before listening—that is his folly and his shame" (Proverbs 18:13), and, "The first to present his case seems right, till another comes forward and questions him" (Proverbs

18:17). Obviously the tendency to reach premature conclusions has been around for a long time.

The Children of Israel were commanded to investigate a certain matter very closely, to "inquire, probe and investigate it thoroughly" before declaring judgment (Deuteronomy 13:12-15). Paul tells Timothy that a charge is not to be brought against an elder without two or three witnesses (I Timothy 5:19).

Be very careful about taking sides in an issue. It is immature to feel that we have to take sides on every issue. We must not allow friends or others to pressure us into something we don't feel is right. God may want us to remain neutral and help promote reconciliation. "Blessed are the peacemakers, for they will be called sons of God" (Matthew 5:9).

4. If there is no change, pray about confronting your leader.

The Bible teaches that we are to go to those who sin against us (Matthew 18:15-20). However, we must be sensitive as to when and how we do this, in order to prevent frustration and hurt on both sides.

Several years ago, I badly hurt a fellow leader. I quickly went to him to make things right, but he turned me away coldly. I followed up with phone calls, letters, and more visits, yet he still refused to soften his attitude towards me. Technically, he forgave me, but our fellowship was not restored.

I began to think that I had done all I possibly could in the situation, and the next move was his. As I sought God, though, I realized I had not gone to him in a prayerful way, with the right preparation of heart. I wasn't sufficiently broken over the hurt and embarrassment I had caused him. I expected him to feel an obligation to forgive me with little effort on my part. I continued to pray for him daily, and several months passed before I sensed the Lord directing me to approach him again. I called, and he reluctantly agreed to meet me. This time, though, my heart was ready, and I wept as I asked his forgiveness; confessing my sin openly to him. The Lord had brought me to such a place that I was willing to do whatever was necessary to restore the relationship.

I sensed that if we were not reconciled this time, permanent damage would be done to our relationship through unforgiveness. As I knelt before him as a sign of my contrition, tears began to trickle down his cheeks. He reached down and embraced me, and together we wept, prayed, laughed, and cried. What a relief and joy it was to be fully restored and reunited in our relationship.

It is a hard and humbling experience to go to someone in this manner, especially if the person is the one who has sinned against us. And what happens if the person doesn't respond? The answer to this depends upon the nature of the problem.

If it is a serious sin—sexual immorality, stealing, or some extreme doctrinal error—then others must be involved. If the leader is truly repentant, he will confess his sin and do whatever is necessary to set the matter right. If he is not repentant, then you must take action to try and rectify the matter. Go to a well-respected pastor or leader outside your immediate situation and seek his or her advice.

In situations where this procedure has not been followed, the problem can escalate out of control. People who do not have anything to contribute to the working out of a solution are dragged in, get hurt, and God's name is dishonored. However, when such situations have been handled in a godly manner, they have been quietly resolved.

Several years ago, I met a pastor who related the following story to me.

He told me how the wife of the pastor who had preceded him had become sexually involved with a man in the church. Finally they ran away together to another town close by, much to the shame of the pastor and the entire congregation. Because of the proximity of the town and the circumstances, it was inevitable that the whole church would soon learn about it. However, this is where the story differs from most.

Rather than indulge in gossip and judgmental conversations about the situation, the church went to prayer. Leading men from the church met regularly with the pastor, and agreed with him in prayer that God would restore his wife. The women of the church began a twenty-four hour prayer chain. Perhaps what showed their love most of all was that the whole story was not spread around town or to the local newspapers. Discussion of the situation was kept to an absolute minimum, while prayer for it was going on continually.

A small delegation of the ladies were sent to find the pastor's wife and communicate their love and concern. They found her staying in a dingy hotel room, and after much pleading, she agreed to go back with them. On her return, a special meeting of the church women was held. Their initial efforts to pray for her were rejected, but after much persistence and many tears, she broke and wept her way back to God and His forgiveness. The love of the church women, their pleading, prayers, understanding and willingness to forgive had finally conquered her rebellious heart.

The pastor resigned from the church to give more time and attention to his badly neglected marriage. Wonderfully, they had been spared the shame of a public scandal. The sin had not been "covered up," it had been "covered over"—covered over by love.

Note the principles followed in handling this situation:

- The pastor's wife was disciplined by having to ask for forgiveness in public. However, the motivation for this was not to punish but to restore. It was done before the women of the church, which spared her the agony of going before the entire congregation. James 5:19-20 speaks about the loving spirit that should always be our motive when dealing with the failure of a brother or sister.

- The situation was handled by those who were mature in the church, and with patience and gentleness (Galatians 6:1-5).

- It was done in stages, and every opportunity was given for the sister to respond (Matthew 18:15-35).

- The women of the church went to visit her with the correct facts and a desire to resolve the problem. The pastor also engaged in much prayer and soul-searching with the elders, and ultimately agreed to promote healing of the situation through resigning his post.

If we go to our leader and he does not receive what we have to share, then we have three choices: go back with another person as a witness and reconciliatory agent; wait, believing God will bring change; or remove ourselves from his leadership by leaving the group.

The one option we do not have is to stay around and gossip, stirring up dissension and rebellion towards those in authority. We are to "strive for peace with all men, and for the holiness without which no one will see the Lord. See to it that no one fail to obtain the grace of God; that no 'root of bitterness' spring up and cause trouble, and by it the many become defiled" (Hebrews 12:14-15, RSV). Gossip and public criticism will lead to our destruction, not theirs: "Do not grumble, brethren, against one another, that you may not be judged; behold, the Judge is standing at the doors. As an example of suffering and patience, brethren, take the prophets. . . ." (James 5:9-10, RSV). In this verse, being patient and enduring suffering is in the context of our behavior towards our brethren, and not unbelievers.

Whatever action is decided upon as best, it must be done in an attitude of love. God will vindicate us in His time if necessary. "If it is possible, as far as it depends on you, live at peace with everyone. Do not take revenge, my friends, but leave room for God's wrath, for it is written: 'It is mine to avenge; I will repay,' says the Lord" (Romans 12:18-19).

King David is a powerful example of a person who waited for God's timing instead of using the methods of his oppressor to force change. When the opportunity arose to kill Saul, he refused to do so, recognizing that Saul was still God's anointed one (I Samuel 24:6). At the same time, he did not give up believing that God had promised him the crown one day, but waited on God to bring it to pass.

There is a difference between standing up to a leader who is wrong, and placing ourselves in the dangerous position of leading a one-man crusade against him. God has allowed the situation to arise, and by moving in our own understanding and strength, we may actually be getting in the way of His greater plans.

Personally, I am extremely grateful that God is so patient. I have made many mistakes as a leader—hurting people, riding over their feelings in my impatience, and even manipulating those who saw things differently from me. I owe an immense debt of gratitude to those who have responded to me in a godly way and kept me on track. I am especially grateful to Loren Cunningham, President of Youth With A Mission, whose trust and belief have allowed me to do things I thought were beyond me. Above all, I am thankful to the Lord who has dusted me off so many times when I have fallen and set me on the path again and again. If only we had that same love and commitment towards one another, instead of treating people harshly in their sin and weakness. We should follow Jesus' example: "A bruised reed he will not break, and a smoldering wick he will not snuff out" (Isaiah 42:3).

Chapter 10

Do You Really Care?

I could hardly believe my eyes — or my ears for that matter. Here stood a little, five-foot-three-inch, pudgy grandfather, mumbling something about my name.

"Are you Floyd McClung, Jr.?" he repeated. I gazed up at him from my study desk in the back corner of the library.

"Yes, I am," I mumbled in return. I was quite taken aback by the shabby appearance of this elderly gentleman, dressed in a very tattered old suit.

"I've been looking for you. God has called me to serve you." He hesitated, and I waited, not knowing what to expect next. "God has called me to be a doormat for you," he concluded.

His name: Pop Jenkins.

His job: Sunday school teacher.

His age: 72.

His role in my life: Doormat.

Rather strange sounding, isn't it? Almost eccentric. Yet it is true.

I was twenty years old, in my second year of theological studies, and rather sold on myself. Don't ask me how he knew my name; I never found out. All I know is that God used him to change my life.

From that strange meeting in the library, my life was intertwined over the next few weeks with that of an "eccentric" old man. It finally culminated in my first "missionary journey."

We traveled several hundred miles south of my parents' home in Southern California to a small village called San Felipe on the Gulf of Mexico.

From the moment we closed the doors on my old 1947 grey Plymouth and set off on our journey, he pestered me with the same question over and over again.

"Do you really care?"

At first it was a bit of a novelty. Then it started sounding serious and spiritual. Finally it got downright annoying. Every ten minutes or so, the same question, "Do you care about people in need? Do you care that people are going to hell? Do you really care?"

Daytime, and an old man walking by the road: "Do you care, Floyd?" Sleeping by the road at night, mosquitoes buzzing in my ears, and Pop Jenkins going on: "Do you really care?"

He questioned everything: my goals, my values, money, sports, motives for ministry—everything. "Do you want to serve God?" he asked. "Why do you want to serve God? Do you really care about people?"

He quietly challenged my relationships, my sense of security, and most important of all, he touched the longing in my heart to serve God.

We stood together in a little cemetery on the top

of a hill, looking down on the village of San Felipe.

"Christian crosses," he said, pointing to the tombstones. "Religious people, dying without Jesus. This is the land of Christless crosses. Do you care, Floyd?"

We visited a church service and watched hundreds of very poor people as they bowed before an icon of a dead priest. Without condemnation, tears quietly flowing down his cheeks. He turned to me and asked once again, "Floyd, do you really care what happens to people?"

Something began to happen inside me. I cried as I watched him put his arms around a drunken man on a dusty road. As he wept and prayed, I saw. I saw a man caring. I realized that here was a man motivated by the love of Christ.

He cared enough to challenge me, cared enough to spend time with me, cared enough to listen to my dreams.

We spent many hours together and we became friends. Now my previous irritation at his constant questioning seemed so petty. Here was a man who cared. He lived his whole life for others. His compassion touched them, changed them. People couldn't remain the same when Pop Jenkins came along.

It was a quiet journey home, that two-day drive from San Felipe. I was tired and dirty. There was dust everywhere. But I was different. A deep longing, an aching desire had been released within me. I desperately wanted what Pop Jenkins had. He cared for people. He had time for them. There was an intensity about his love for people that was annoying to anyone superficial in his Christian faith. He was single-minded. He was serious. He cared. He loved people.

That trip to Mexico was my first trip to another land — my first missionary journey. Since then I have traveled on every continent and visited over one hundred nations. Even though that trip with Pop Jenkins was the shortest, and perhaps the strangest, it was the most memorable. It spoiled me for the ordinary.

It is love that will change the world. It is important to dedicate ourselves to God's service, but it is love that reveals how genuine our dedication is. It is absolutely essential to pray as a Christian, but it is love that puts feet to our prayers. We must be willing and ready to be part of the answer to our prayers. It is imperative that we experience revival in our nation, but revival without love is only a spurious experience. Only a revival of love will transform a nation.

God's love changes people — it is the greatest power in the world. Are you ready to lay down your life for others? Are you prepared to put your words into action? Are you serious enough to do what you sing about on Sunday? Are you willing to do it out of love? Love that trusts? Love that accepts? Love that heals? Love that forgives? Love that encourages?

Do you really care?

Unity Between the Local Church and Other Structures

There are two streams in church history. The first deals with the preaching of the Gospel to every tribe and nation (Matthew 28:18-20); the second deals with the maturing of the saints to be salt and light in a fallen world (Ephesians 3 and 4).

At times these two streams have blended together without tension; at other times they have shown little or no sense of accountability nor respect towards one another.

Called by different names—the "order" and the "parish," the "mobile church" and the "local church," the "missionary society" and the "denomination," the "apostolic band" and the "local assembly"—the tension is the same, and quite universal.

While the local church or parish is strongly committed to seeing its people becoming established and taking positions of leadership and responsibility, the missionary organization is just as committed to challenging those same saints with God's call to go into all the world and preach the Gospel to every creature.

This natural tension is heightened, in some circles, by the teaching that the local church is the ideal structure and the only truly biblical expression of the Body of Christ. When the local church does its job, the need for the missionary society will be non-existent, so it is said.

In some streams of the Charismatic renewal, this teaching has gone so far as to say that in each town there is one anointed church around which all the other churches in that town will eventually gather, somehow becoming an extension of that one "anointed" body.

Others believe in missions, but are strongly convinced that all missionary activity should *only* be done through the auspices of the local church. They see the biblical pattern as being one of raising up apostolic church-planting teams, comprising only well-proven ministries. These teams should be subject to the authority of the local church, no matter how far away they go or how specialized their task.

At the opposite end of the spectrum, there seems to be a lack of accountability on the part of some missionary societies. The tendency is to feel there is no need to refer to the local church; that if a parishioner wants to join a mission agency, then that is between him or her and the Lord.

These missionary organizations believe the local church member is accountable only to God for what he does. Though he should inform the pastor or priest of his intentions, he does not need to submit to him fully — especially if the pastor is against missionary organizations. The local church tends to be regarded as a place to recruit people and raise money. In this view, the local church should merely train people, send them, support them, and receive them back home when they are tired or needy. There is no real relationship between the mission leaders and the pastor of the local church. Many pastors feel they have virtually no voice in who is recruited from their church.

The tension examined

Part of the historical tension between the local church and the missionary society has been that, on the one hand, the local church does not want all its resources depleted. On the other hand, the missionary society does not want to lose autonomy by being totally under the authority of a local assembly.

The purpose of this appendix is to appeal to church and mission leaders and to all concerned laymen, to recognize the dangers in allowing this tension to continue. We must address the issues in a humble and open manner. The Church today has never faced greater opportunities, but an unresolved conflict between these two streams will undermine our efforts to respond to the opportunities we have to witness to the world.

We need each other. God has created the Church both to nurture local believers and to reach out to a lost world. Local churches and missionary movements that share a spirit of mutual accountability and cooperation will be able to participate in one of the greatest thrusts forward in church history. We are on the threshold of a new surge of church growth, and God is preparing us to be a prophetic voice to the nations. This is the century of the Holy Spirit, and the century is not over yet—the best is yet to come. I believe powerful evangelism is about to rejuvenate the Church worldwide in ways we never thought possible.

It is absolutely essential that we act together if we are to see this growth come about. Several important adjustments need to be made in our attitudes and theology in order to allow the Church to be the powerful united force God intends it to be.

(1) We must renounce all attitudes of independence and pride. Any attitude that suggests that our group or church does not need the rest of the Body of Christ, or makes us feel we are the precursors of the Kingdom of God in and of ourselves, or that we alone are at the center of what God is doing, is pride. God is at work through many different groups and churches, and through many church structures.

Any response to other Christians that does not promote unity, no matter how wrong we feel they are, is sin. When missionary and evangelistic organizations act independently of established and local churches, they only reinforce the worst fears of those church leaders. You do not conquer one perceived wrong with another.

(2) We need to develop a much more positive and dynamic ecclesiology (the study of church structure). If our view of the Church is too exclusive, it will result in ignoring or even denying God's blessing on many structures outside the local church. If our view of the local church is negative, it will result in a lack of love and enthusiasm for what God is doing in a particular town or city.

I love the Church! And God loves the Church, too! It is alive, dynamic, growing, and powerful. The Church is God's work—in all its forms and in all its ministries.

The Church is the wine, and church structures are the wineskins. Although the wineskins change, the wine does not. While church structures change according to culture, men's giftings, and what God is doing in a particular nation or group change, the fact that redeemed people make up the community of God never changes.

God is not a God of methods and formulas, restricted to certain ways of working. While He has used the Anglican Church in Singapore (every parish has experienced radical renewal), in a certain nation of the Middle East, He has used a mission hospital. He is using translation teams as the key to revival in some Asian nations, and at the same time He is using prayer groups to touch the capital city of a major Western nation. What works in one place may not work in another. The Holy Spirit is like a wind that cannot be contained in any man's box. The Church is so dynamic that it cannot be controlled by the theology of any one group.

Missionary movements such as Campus Crusade for Christ, Youth With A Mission, and Wycliffe Bible Translators have experienced great growth and blessing in the past two decades. Between these three groups, 73,000 full- and part-time workers were mobilized in 1985 alone, and through their ministries over 2.1 million people indicated they wanted to accept Jesus Christ as their Lord and Savior. In Youth With A Mission, new churches are being established among unreached peoples on an average of one every day. Youth With A Mission is entering a new nation with a permanent work every three weeks. God has been so good!

It is important to recognize the blessing on these groups—it is God's way of commending them to the wider Church. But those of us in missionary organizations also need to recognize our need of local churches and parishes.

As a leader of a missionary movement, it is my desire for us to be fully supportive of local church missions. I want to serve local churches and parishes and help them become the powerful, growing churches their pastors long for them to be. I also want to be accountable to those churches. I believe that as I choose this attitude, and as it is reflected in the actions of our mission, I can help break down the barriers that separate us.

(3) In order to be the united force God wants us to be, both local churches and missionary organizations need to accept their limitations and the complementary relationship God intends them to have with one another.

Local churches are best at equipping new believers and nourishing them as they serve as salt and light in society. And missionary organizations know how to train people for cross-cultural service. Accepting our limitations and the dependency we have upon one another allows us to inspire and replenish one another.

Each dimension of the Church—local and missionary—has a particular calling. Fulfilling these callings creates a cycle of interdependent activities and mutual blessing. A missionary team goes to an unreached group of people, makes converts, and starts a new fellowship. The new fellowship, in turn, sends out another team which carries out evangelism resulting in new church life, and so the cycle continues.

In many situations we need missionary teams that do not start new churches but work within established churches to bring renewal. As they equip newly committed Christians to share their faith with others, they are fulfilling the Great Commission as much as if they had started a new church.

(4) Local churches must not see the Great Commission as an addendum to the church program. It must be *the* church program. It is not an optional extra, but the driving force and central vision of the Church.

How then, does the Great Commission affect the relationship between the local church and the missionary society? If a local church does not view the Great Commission as central to all its activities, it will be in a constant struggle with those who do. Those people will feel torn between their commitment to the local church and to missions. But if the local church is consumed with a desire for world evangelization, there is no occasion for divided loyalties among its members.

Missions is then a matter of calling, and taking time to test that calling. If a person is called into missionary service, it is only reasonable to expect them to be active in the church's local evangelistic activities. Failure to provide these activities is to invite a crisis of loyalty. (This is especially true for young people.) However, we should not regard these activities as ways to "keep" more people in the church. The church should joyfully embrace the task of training its best to go to other cities and other lands. To hold onto people is to lose them in the long run.

Why not develop a positive, well-thought-out program which will develop those qualities needed for missionary work, rather than forcing people to feel rebellious for wanting to step out in any form of Christian service outside the local church? A church with this generosity of spirit and broadness of vision will always be flooded with new people because God can entrust them to its care. A church must view obedience to the Great Commission as an extension of its own health as a body. Indeed, a church cannot consider itself truly renewed or restored if it does not have this view of the Great Commission.

(5) Local churches and missionary organizations should develop well-thought-out policies of how they will relate to each other and what they expect of one another. Establishing mission committees and/or appointing a particular person to be responsible for missions in the local church will help channel those who want to serve. The church that does not make missions its future has no real future. The future of both the Church and the world is to love the whole world with God's love. To love the world in this sacrificial way is absolutely essential if we are going to be instruments in God's hands to see it changed.

For more information on how to establish a missions committee and to form missions' policies in the local church, please write to:

Youth With A Mission
Attn: Personnel Department
Prins Hendrikkade 50
1012 AC Amsterdam
The Netherlands

STUDY
GUIDE

STUDY GUIDE: Chapter 1

For Personal Study

- In what instances—or from whom—have I experienced accepting love on a human level? How did it affect my life?

- Among the people I encounter regularly, who especially needs to receive accepting love from me? How can I show such love to this person(s)?

- What has been my response when someone has genuinely trusted me—even when I haven't earned such trust?

- Is there a person in my life to whom I need to convey trusting love? When and how should I go about doing so?

- In what difficult area of my life do I need to appropriate God's healing love?

- To whom in my circle of relationships should I begin to channel God's healing love? In what specific way can I do this during the next week?

For Group Discussion

• Why can accepting love be so powerful?

• What are some visible characteristics of accepting love?

• How is accepting love consistent with the Gospel of Christ?

• Why is accepting love difficult to practice?

• Why is trust "the key that can unlock a person's full potential"?

• Why is God's healing love able to remedy deep-seated personal problems when even counseling and personal discipline seem fruitless?

• What effect would an atmosphere of accepting love, trusting love, and healing love have on the relationships within our local body of believers?

STUDY GUIDE: Chapter 2

For Personal Study

- What kinds of people have I found difficult to view as my equals in Christ? Why have I felt uncomfortable with these people?

- In my local "universe," to which group of believers do I need to begin reaching out in order to affirm our oneness in Christ (even though I don't fully agree with them)?

- Regarding differences among Christians, which matters do I consider essential, and which do I consider nonessential?

- Is my personal list of "essentials" based on biblical truth, or on personal comfort? How do I know this?

- When have I allowed legalism or liberalism to substitute for true Christian unity? How can I best avoid either of these errors?

For Group Discussion

• Why do racial, social, political, and theological differences often pose great barriers to Christian unity?

• What are some of the most common issues that tend to divide Christians?

• Within our own body of believers, what issues might pose barriers to genuine love and unity?

• When a group exhibits a great deal of diversity, what will be the signs of being "one in Christ"?

• What are genuine essentials of the Christian faith? Why are they so important?

• What are some nonessentials that often slip into the "essential" category? Why are they often considered so important?

• Why do both legalism and liberalism create false unity? How can we as a body of believers prevent these errors from diluting our fellowship?

• How is it possible to maintain a biblical standard and yet be loving?

• Why is sin such an effective "equalizer"? And why is the cross the key to unity?

STUDY GUIDE: Chapter 3

For Personal Study

- Do my relationships at church, at home, and elsewhere reveal a pattern of love and unity? An opposite pattern? Why?

- In what instances have I been disappointed by another believer(s)? What effect did that disappointment have on my relationship with Christ and other believers?

- What can I be doing and thinking to prevent another believer's failure from derailing my own spiritual progress?

- What will happen in my personal and church life if I consciously give up my rights for the sake of Christian unity?

For Group Discussion

• What is the reason for the maxim, "If you have one believer you have a Christian, if you have two believers you have a church, and if you have three believers you have two churches"? Why do churches seem to hold such great potential for disunity?

• If unity does not come automatically in marriage or other relationships, what should we do to build such unity?

• Why do we tend to idealize fellow believers (particularly leaders) and figuratively put them on pedestals? Why is this a harmful attitude?

• If we are incapable of changing other people and their attitudes, how can we help bring about unity with them?

• Why is the issue of marriage and divorce so important to unity within the body of believers?

• What is the practical significance of Jesus' prayer for unity in John 17?

• What does the author mean by writing, "No one who participates in division is right"?

• Discuss the nature of love as revealed in John 15: 13-17. How will obedience to Jesus' command transform our lives together?

STUDY GUIDE: Chapter 4

For Personal Study

- How do I usually feel toward another believer if I see (or hear about) that person committing sin or failing?

- Am I *eager* to maintain the unity of the Spirit in my relationships with other believers? How do I know this?

- How do I make sure that I am speaking the truth *in love* when dealing with other believers?

- Am I harboring wrong attitudes toward any group or individual because of information I have received "second-hand"? If so, what should I do to heal this broken relationship?

- How do my actions and attitudes toward other believers show that I am filled (or not filled) with the Holy Spirit?

For Group Discussion

• What is the difference between "unity of the Spirit" and "unity of the faith"?

• Why is unity of the Spirit so crucial to our relationships?

• Why does God want each of us to judge our own heart and life rather than others' hearts and lives?

• What is the difference between speaking the truth in love and merely speaking the truth?

• Why does speaking the truth not necessarily edify the other person?

• Why should we forgive a believer who is wrong, even if that person refuses to repent? How can we forgive in such an instance?

• If "God does not reveal all His truth to any one person or Christian group," how should we act toward one another?

STUDY GUIDE: Chapter 5

For Personal Study

- Among the people I deal with, which one do I find most difficult–even impossible–to love?

- If I were Corrie ten Boom and were facing that former SS prison guard, how would I react to his outstretched hand and acknowledgment of God's forgiveness? (Be honest!)

- What am I like in my most unlovable moments? How does this compare to the behavior of people I consider unlovable?

- Who in my life am I having difficulty forgiving? How can I persist in forgiveness until I truly feel love for that person?

For Group Discussion

• Why does real love seem to "cut against the grain of our fallen nature"?

• Why should we forgive someone even if that person doesn't deserve our forgiveness?

• How can we fulfill God's command to love people, even if such love seems humanly impossible?

• Why do we often struggle with truly forgiving someone who has wronged us?

• Why is forgiveness sometimes a process rather than just a single, simple act?

• Why is "moving toward" a person an effective key to healing a broken relationship? Why is it so difficult?

• What are some methods of establishing dialogue with someone when the relationship has been breached?

• How can we best prevent or check the spreading of negative words about another believer?

STUDY GUIDE: Chapter 6

For Personal Study

• In what areas of my life am I most prone to jealousy? Why?

• How has jealousy affected my relationships with people, especially other believers? What situation in particular best illustrates this?

• What has God used to reveal pride in my life and to help me gain freedom from it?

• Is there a situation from my past that still calls for restitution? If so, how can I begin to restore the relationship I have helped to damage?

• If busyness is hindering deep relationships in my life, how can I evaluate my priorities and begin to reorder them?

For Group Discussion

- What are possible causes of jealousy among believers?

- Are there measures we as a body can take to reduce the possibility of jealousy among us?

- What are some ways in which pride (personal and corporate) can display itself among believers?

- How is pride among Christians sometimes rationalized?

- What might be some effective ways in which to confront a believer with an obvious pride problem?

- Why is independence a "great curse on spiritual unity"?

- Is the concept of restitution and forgiveness very visible among today's Christians? Why?

- Why is the hindrance of busyness so prevalent in Western culture? How can we take precautions against this tendency?

For Personal Study

• What kinds of people do I consider the most difficult? Why?

• If a fellow believer falls into sin, how do I usually respond? Is this response biblical?

• Is there a type of manipulative behavior that I sometimes use? Why do I use it?

• How should I go about breaking a habit of manipulative behavior?

• Do I find it easy to talk publicly about my disagreements with another believer? How might such talk be affecting the body of Christ? How should I change my behavior?

For Group Discussion

• Why does real love refuse to compromise on God's principles of holiness?

• Why can manipulative behavior be extremely effective among Christians?

• In what ways can a power manipulator affect a body of believers? How can such manipulation be identified?

• Why do we as Christians sometimes have difficulty confronting a person about manipulative behavior?

• What are some steps to take when confronting manipulative behavior? Why are these steps important?

• Why is it crucial that we "make decisions that are based on principles and not pressure"?

• What are the dangers of publicly condemning believers because we do not agree with some of their doctrines or practices? How should we deal with such disagreements?

• How will our relationships be changed if we each try to correct another believer's error by being "personally and redemptively involved with him"?

STUDY GUIDE: Chapter 8

For Personal Study

• Which group decision-making approach do I tend to favor (competitive, conflictive, constructive, cop-out, or cooperative)? Am I usually pleased with the results? Why or why not?

• Can I recall an instance in which another believer and I disagreed about an important issue, yet our fellowship remained unbroken? Can I recall a time when disagreement had the opposite result? What made the difference?

• How would I describe the level of my commitment to other Christians in the local body?

• How do I encourage my leaders to properly fulfill their responsibilities?

• If I am in leadership, how do I make sure that I am properly carrying out my responsibilities rather than abusing my position?

For Group Discussion

- In our own body of believers, do we often resort to one style of decision-making over others (competitive, conflictive, constructive, cop-out, or cooperative)? Why?

- Why is commitment to one another crucial to the success of cooperative decision-making?

- How can we ensure that our leaders will carry out their roles in a responsible, godly manner?

- What can we as a body do to create a climate of good personal relationships among believers?

- Do we as a body share a unified vision? If so, what is that vision? How did this sharing of vision come to be?

- In our life as a body of believers, what does it mean to have a submissive heart?

- How can we as believers be unified, even if we disagree on certain issues?

- How is good communication cultivated in a group of believers?

STUDY GUIDE: Chapter 9

For Personal Study

• What is my usual attitude toward leaders? Why?

• Have I ever been deeply disappointed by a Christian leader? How has that event affected my relationship with the church and its leaders?

• How do I tend to react when a leader is doing something that I consider wrong? What effect does my reaction have on other people, as well as on my own spiritual life?

• How much effort do I devote to praying for my leaders? Am I satisfied with this level of prayer support?

• Can I recall any instances in which I or someone else accused a leader before knowing all the facts? What were the results of such wrongful accusation?

For Group Discussion

• What are some of the pressures that a Christian leader faces?

• How can we, as members of a body, reduce some of the pressures our leaders face?

• What should we do if a leader does not respect the people under him? How can we help prevent a leader from falling into this attitude?

• If a leader has truly fallen, what are some important principles to follow in dealing with the problem?

• How is it possible to "disobey a leader submissively"?

• What is wrong with the assertion that a "spiritual person" knows it is wrong to correct a leader?

• If character is the "qualification needed for someone to challenge or correct a leader," what are the marks of such character?

• How can someone objectively confront a leader if he or she has been deeply hurt by that leader?

• How can we protect leaders from being wrongfully accused by well-meaning people who have gained false or incomplete information?

• What should be our goal when confronting a leader about alleged wrongdoing?

STUDY GUIDE: Chapter 10

For Personal Study

• How would I have reacted to Pop Jenkins' offer to be a "doormat"?

• If Jenkins were to ask me, "Do you really care?" what would be my honest response?

• Is my love strong enough to trust, accept, heal, forgive, and encourage anyone that needs my love? How do I know?

For Group Discussion

• Why did Pop Jenkins continually badger the author with the question, "Do you really care?"

• What was the result of Jenkins' repeated "Do you care?"

• How was Jenkins' assertive behavior consistent with his offer to be a "doormat"?

• In a world that is swayed by economic and military might, how can the author assert that "love will change the world"?

• Why is love the only characteristic that will reveal the genuineness of our dedication to the cause of Christ?

• Is it possible to have "revival without love" as described by the author? Why or why not?

STUDY GUIDE: APPENDIX

For Personal Study

• What is my general concept of what God's Church should be? Is this concept shared by others in my circle of fellowship? How do I personally contribute toward making that concept a reality?

• How would I rate the importance of the Great Commission in my own life? In my local church's life?

• How can my personal priorities be changed to enhance the focus on the Great Commission in my local church fellowship?

For Group Discussion

• What is required for "the Church to be the powerful united force God intends it to be"?

• Why are independence and pride (individual or corporate) so damaging to the progress of the Kingdom of God?

• What concepts will help build a "more positive and dynamic" view of church structure?

• What kind of people make up the community of God? How should this affect our attitudes toward one another?

• As a fellowship of believers, are we realistic about our group's strengths and limitations? What steps have we taken to build complementary relationships with other Christian bodies?

• What is the place of the Great Commission in the program and strategy of our local body? Do we agree that it has an adequate place of priority?

• How can placing a high priority on the Great Commission help to prevent "divided loyalties" among church members?

• How can a church take a proactive stance in relating to independent missionary organizations?

About the Author

Floyd McClung, Jr. is the founder and director of Mission Village in Trinidad, Colorado. Mission Village is a growing community of training and outreach ministries committed to raising up a new generation of young world-changers for Jesus.

Mission Village sponsors one-year youth leadership schools, discipleship and evangelism schools, biblical studies programs, short-term outreaches, sports and outdoor adventure opportunities, drama teams, and many other exciting programs that are reaching, equipping, and mobilizing a vast army of young men and women to reach the world for Christ.

If you would like more information about how you can become part of Mission Village or attend one of the training schools offered at Mission Village, write today to:

Mission Village
P.O. Box 5
Trinidad, CO 81082
USA